Yankee Surveyors
in the Shogun's Seas

Yankee Surveyors
in the Shogun's Seas

Records of the
United States Surveying Expedition
to the North Pacific Ocean,
1853-1856

EDITED BY ALLAN B. COLE

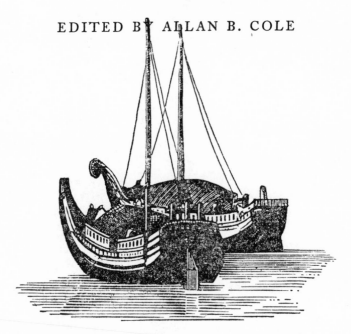

GREENWOOD PRESS, PUBLISHERS
NEW YORK

Background of the Surveying Expedition

Background of the Surveying Expedition

Now that the recent battles in the violent Pacific are over, now that the Japanese Empire has collapsed, thoughts are turning toward the future, in anxiety for a lasting peace—and toward the past, to ascertain the factors which contributed toward the conflict. Part of this trend is an inquiry through the fogs of prejudice and propaganda into historical events in an attempt to assess responsibility for aggression and war. This is more than a futile indoor sport. It is part of the human quest for morality and law among nations. More narrowly it becomes an intellectual form of national defense.

Let us take, for example, the Japanese attack on Pearl Harbor. It was "unprovoked," says the official statement of the United States government. "We cannot agree," say the dissenters, including presumably most of seventy-five million Japanese, "what about the A-B-C-D blockade of Japan in August before that fateful December 7th? That was a declaration of white warfare."

"But the blockade was long delayed; it was described as a measure 'short of war,' and it was provoked by Japanese aggression as far as Indo-China. . . ." And so the debate turns to the history of the basic issues of the war and the growth of national policies. Pressed backward through nine decades of American-Japanese relations the protagonists face each other, still in disagreement, over the nature and consequences of the United States naval expedition under Commodore Matthew C. Perry which reopened Japan to intercourse with the West. Was it, as Perry himself and most of his countrymen have since maintained, a friendly mission with objectives beneficial to Japan as well as to occidental commerce? Or was it a modified naval invasion of Japanese security, resulting in a semi-colonial status from which Japan could escape only by adopting the power-policies of the aggressors?

The letters here published provide evidence on this issue. They furnish eye-witness accounts of the attitudes of ordinary and official Japanese meeting the first American merchants, sailors, and naval officers who followed Perry to test the effectiveness of his Treaty of Kanagawa (March 31, 1854), which had opened the ports of Shimoda and Hakodaté for limited trade. Indeed, this was one of the primary objectives set by the Navy Department for the major but undeservedly forgotten United States Surveying Expedition to the North Pacific Ocean.

Not only was this expedition instructed by Secretary of the Navy John P. Kennedy to implement the recent treaty; it was also to chart trans-Pacific routes over which steamships might soon churn from booming San Francisco around the Great Circle to Asia or directly to the Sandwich Islands (Hawaii), to seclusive Nagasaki (where coal was said to abound), and on to bustling Shanghai. Moreover, the rugged Japanese archipelago together with the island chains to south and north were hazardous for the hundreds of whaling ships which hunted in these waters as far north as the Bering Sea. Lieutenant Matthew Fontaine Maury of the National Observatory had recently charted a course by which scores of merchantmen plying between California and the Far East could reduce the time of passage by one week. Agitation by American merchants and their captains led Secretary William A. Graham, Kennedy's predecessor, to state in a letter to the Speaker of the Senate (April 5, 1852) that in addition to the Perry expedition, then being prepared, another force should be dispatched to explore waters around and north of China and Japan, which were becoming "every day of more and more importance." The appropriating House was similarly urged and on August 31, 1852, responded by allocating $125,000 "for prosecuting a survey and reconnaissance for naval and commercial purposes, of such parts of Behrings Straits, of the North Pacific Ocean and of the China Seas, as are frequented by American whaleships and by trading vessels in their routes between the United States and China."

Five ships were commissioned for the enterprise, and since the letters presented here were written aboard three of them, we may pause for descriptions. Flagship of this expedition, as of that better known venture to the Antarctic and Pacific (1838-42) under Lieutenant Charles Wilkes, was the 700-ton sloop-of-war *Vincennes*. In her quarter century of service she had frequently carried her eighteen guns into Far Eastern seas.[1] The bark-rigged tender *John Hancock*, two guns, was the only steamer in the squadron.[2] A 350-ton merchantman was purchased at New York and converted into a naval storeship renamed the *John P. Kennedy*.[3] When new, the brig *Porpoise* had circumnavigated the globe on the Wilkes expedition under Cadwalader Ringgold, who now commanded the surveying squadron. She displaced 224 tons and carried ten guns with a crew of eighty.[4] Last and smallest was the 95-ton schooner *Fenimore Cooper*, which sailed as a tender.

[1] Length between perpendiculars: 127 feet; beam moulded: 33 feet, 9 inches; depth of hold: 15 feet, 6 inches; maximum draft: 16 feet, 6 inches.
[2] Length: 151 feet; beam: 22 feet; depth: 14 feet; cost: $112,560.84.
[3] Her bow had been inscribed *Sea Nymph*. She cost the Navy $25,000. In June 1854, the *John P. Kennedy* was undergoing repairs at Hongkong; in August she was detached from the surveying expedition and stationed near Canton, where she remained until October 1855. In the next month she was sold for $10,000.
[4] Length: 88 feet; beam: 25 feet; depth: 11 feet.

Scientific observations were to be major activities for both expeditions: the surveying venture was timed so as to supplement the diplomatic mission under Perry. Both recruited personnel from scientists who had charted the Atlantic and Pacific coasts of the United States and had served in waters off every continent. Lieutenant John M. Brooke, as astronomer for the North Pacific expedition, also employed the sounding lead which had proved effective in preparing the route for the trans-Atlantic cable; off Japanese shores it brought up samples of ocean floor from depths as great as 3,500 fathoms.[5]

Scientists with both squadrons borrowed instruments and libraries from the National Observatory. They became familiar with the discoveries of such navigators as Krusenstern, Golovnin, Broughton, and La Perouse; they also learned of the experiences of that succession of physicians and agents who had served the Dutch commercial monopoly on the guarded islet of Deshima in Nagasaki Bay. There, since 1641, only Netherlanders of all Westerners had been permitted by the Tōkugawa shogunate to trade. Engelbrecht Kaempfer, Carl Peter Thunberg, Isaac Titsingh, Hendrick Doeff, J. F. van O. Fischer, G. F. Meylan, and J. P. F. von Siebold had provided much information. The last mentioned had smuggled out of Deshima a copy of Inō Chukei's famous map of Nippon, which had been engraved in 1823; copies of this aided the Americans.

Commander Ringgold was also supplied with a 460-page treatise on commercial and scientific aspects of the Far East which had been compiled by Aaron H. Palmer, a promoter and commission merchant of New York. In addition, both he and Perry received copies of a letter penned by Commander James Glynn in 1850 after his warship, the *Preble*, had rescued American whalingmen who had been stranded in Japan. It read in part:

[5] Americans already were proposing a trans-Pacific cable which, with projected telegraph lines across Siberia, would girdle the globe with telecommunications.

There is a portion of the ocean inclosed by lines drawn from Cape Awa, the South-eastern point of Japan, Southerly to the Bonin Islands; thence to the Southern point of Formosa; then from the Northern point of Formosa to Cape Gotto, and along the Southern shore of Japan, which offers an interesting field for original discovery, or a re-survey by the improved means of the present day, and which assumes an uncommon interest to the people of the United States, when taken in connection with the probability that it will soon become the preferred route of the immense commerce that is now anticipated to grow up between the Eastern Coasts of Asia and the Western coast of America. . . . Within this defined space, too, will probably be found the most desirable Depot for coals, when a line of Steamers is established between China and California.[6]

Secretary Kennedy further explained to Ringgold that his expedition was "not for conquest but discovery. Its objects are all peaceful, they are to extend the empire of commerce and of science; to diminish the hazards of the ocean. . . ." Force might be utilized only in self-defense or in the protection of the squadron's property.[7] The public and press fell to speculating about the possible influence of this new project: it might hasten a Pacific steamship line and assert American interests in the Hawaiian Kingdom; added to Perry's squadron it might form a fleet of sixteen or seventeen warships and a total force of perhaps four thousand men.

Cadwalader Ringgold and his command of five ships sailed from Hampton Roads on June 11, 1853. Keeping fairly well together, they stopped at the Madeira and Cape Verde Islands en route to the African Cape and Simons Bay. Weighing anchors in late October to early November, the vessels parted, the flagship with the *Porpoise* sailing parallel courses across the Indian Ocean and around southern Australia to Sydney, arriving on the day after Christmas.[8] About the same time, the

[6] Written to Thomas Ap. Catesby Jones, Commodore of the Pacific Squadron, from Benicia, California, February 21, 1850; see *Pacific Squadron Letters* (MS).

[7] Secretary Kennedy to Commander Ringgold, Washington, February 28, 1853, in *Confidential Letters, No. 3* (February 1, 1853—October 17, 1857), pp. 14-21 (MS).

[8] The *Porpoise* usually ran between the south latitudes 38° and 45° and

other three vessels arrived at Batavia, Java, via the Sunda Strait. The first four months of the new year (1854) were spent by the *Hancock* and *Kennedy* charting the Gaspar and Karimata Straits and the archipelagoes between Java and Singapore. From that British base they reached Hongkong late in May. The *Cooper* worked more directly northward through minor archipelagoes and the South China Sea, arriving at the rendezvous nearly a month later. The two vessels from Sydney had made Hongkong by March 17th to 20th. Both had sailed through the Coral Sea; the *Vincennes*, farther east, visited the Santa Cruz Islands while the *Porpoise* rounded the eastern end of New Guinea. Each passed through the Carolines and touched at Guam before heading for Hongkong via the Bashee group.

The ensuing year was marked by delays and confusion in the squadron. When Perry's mission in January had made its second departure for Edo (now Tōkyō) Bay, the Commodore had left few vessels to protect American interests along the Chinese coasts from disorders accompanying the T'ai P'ing Rebellion. So, after repairs, the storeship *John P. Kennedy* joined the East India Squadron and was stationed at Canton.

Disease and liquor were demoralizing the crews and command. Ringgold himself was attacked by a fever which caused a temporary mental break-down, and for a time there was chaos in administration of the expedition. In August 1854 a board of naval physicians, acting under Commodore Perry's directive, declared Ringgold unfit for active service; his duties devolved upon Lieutenant John Rodgers, who left the *John Hancock* to Lieutenant Henry K. Stevens in order to assume flag duties aboard the *Vincennes* after August 11th.

At this point the letters become interesting, and now for the first time a selection of them is published. Since reports on voyages were occasionally delayed, their sequence has sometimes been slightly altered for the sake of a smoother narra-

---

passed through Bass Strait; the *Vincennes* preferred the course between 42° and 50° 5′ and sailed south of Tasmania.

tive. Because the principal reports which compose our story were written by the four commanders, John Rodgers, Henry Stevens, William Gibson, and John Brooke, it is appropriate to pause for comment on their experience.

John Rodgers was born in Maryland on August 8, 1812. He joined the Navy at the age of sixteen, and before serving with the North Pacific expedition he had been attached twice to the Mediterranean Squadron, once to the Brazil Squadron, and three times to coastal surveys. He later served with distinction in the Civil War; as a rear-admiral he commanded the Asiatic Fleet in 1870-72, and in 1877 he was appointed Superintendent of the National Observatory, where he died on May 5, 1882. The frontispiece shows Rear Admiral John Rodgers later in life. From this portrait, but still more from his letters, we can believe the comments of his contemporaries: that he combined the traits of aggressive vigor, tenacity, and ambition with frankness, patience, and calm judgment.[9]

Henry K. Stevens was born in Connecticut on October 17, 1824. He was appointed as a midshipman from Florida when still under fifteen years of age. Before assignment to the exploring expedition, he had served twice with the Pacific and twice with the Brazil Squadron. While still a lieutenant he joined the Confederate States Navy in 1861.

William Gibson (1825-1887) was born in Baltimore and, at the age of sixteen, was appointed from Pennsylvania as a midshipman. Before serving under Ringgold and Rodgers, he had cruised with United States squadrons off Brazil and in the Mediterranean; from 1849 to 1852 he had been engaged with the Coast Survey. After returning from the North Pacific, Gibson spent two years in Washington organizing materials, and in 1859 after another expedition to Paraguay he returned

[9] See an obituary in the *Army and Navy Journal* (May 13, 1882), p. 936; J. Russell Soley, "Rear-Admiral John Rodgers, President of the Naval Institute, 1879-82," *U.S. Naval Institute Proceedings*, VIII, No. 2 (1882), pp. 251-265; Asaph Hall, "Biographical Memoir of John Rodgers, 1812-1882," *National Academy of Sciences, Biographical Memoirs*, VI (1909), pp. 81-92; *Dictionary of American Biography*, XVI, pp. 77-79; two memoranda in the Office of Naval Records and Library, The National Archives.

to this scientific work. During the Civil War he served in the United States Navy, and before retirement in 1887, he worked at the Hydrographic Office as a full commander.[10]

John M. Brooke was probably the most distinguished naval scientist on the expedition; at least he ultimately won high distinction. Phases of his career will be described elsewhere in these pages, so a few supplementary facts will here suffice. Brooke was born in Florida on December 18, 1826, but he was appointed a midshipman from Virginia in 1841. He had served with the Pacific, Brazil, Mediterranean, and African Squadrons before being assigned to the *Vincennes* for surveying in the North Pacific. He had also worked on the Coast Survey and for more than a year at the Naval Observatory.[11]

Early in September, 1854 (just after Ringgold's departure from Hongkong on the steamer *Susquehanna*), the *Hancock*, often towing the *Cooper*, was assigned to carry Commissioner Robert M. McLane and Secretary of the Legation Dr. Peter Parker from Shanghai to negotiations in North China where they, together with British and French representatives, intended to ask for revision of the treaties with China signed in 1842-44. Visiting Foochow, Shanghai, and arriving at the mouth of the Peiho on October 15th, the vessels anchored for several days until the envoys were officially received. So unsatisfactory were the negotiations that the commissioners became convinced that only military force could improve their status in relations with the Middle Kingdom.[12] The commanders of the American steamer and schooner found opportunities to sound around the mouths of the Min, Huangp'u, Yangtze, Yellow, and Pei rivers; they also reconnoitered in the Gulf of Pechihli. After returning their charges to Shang-

[10] Biographical information on Stevens and Gibson has been taken from memoranda secured in the Office of Naval Records and Library, The National Archives.

[11] This information was also obtained from a memorandum secured from the Office of Naval Records and Library, as well as from the article on John M. Brooke in the *Dictionary of American Biography*, III, pp. 69-70.

[12] Cf. H. B. Morse and H. F. MacNair, *Far Eastern International Relations*. Boston, Houghton Mifflin Company, 1931, pp. 158-159.

hai, they struck out for northern Formosa, examined sections of that island's eastern coast, especially some coal mines in the region, and found the flagship safe at Hongkong in mid-February 1855.

The *Porpoise* and *Vincennes* also had weighed anchor at Hongkong in the previous September. Commander Rodgers last saw the gallant brig as they passed between Formosa and the mainland on September 21st. Her loss, probably in an October typhoon, left three vessels in the expedition. The flagship explored the Bonin (Ōgasawara) and nearby Coffin Islands before turning westward to Naha, which had been a secondary base for Perry. Failing to meet the *Porpoise*, Rodgers continued to chart single islands and groups between Great Liu Ch'iu (Ōkinawa) and the Bay of Kagōshima, an indentation of the main southern Japanese island of Kyūshū. Here, off the town of Yamagawa, he addressed an amusing letter to a hypothetical Nipponese "Secretary of State for Foreign Affairs," explaining why Americans now found it imperative to examine the coasts of Japan and, in the manner of Perry, promising to renew these investigations in the ensuing season.

Back in Hongkong (by January 30, 1855), Commander Rodgers studied charts made by Perry's draftsmen and forwarded some from his own squadron to Washington. He was preparing for major operations: the charting of both coasts of Japan and explorations northward into Bering Sea and along the Aleutians. A brig named *Greta* from Hamburg was chartered for $5,000 to carry coal and provisions to the northern Japanese treaty-port and squadron rendezvous of Hakodaté, on the island of Ezo (Hokkaidō). Her captain was directed to fly the American flag in Japanese waters.

Late in February 1855 the *John Hancock* steamed from Hongkong on the real adventure, to be followed in order by the schooner and the flagship by early April. This book contains the principal reports from the ships' commanders to Flag-Officer Rodgers, and from him to Secretary of the Navy James C. Dobbin. Although they tell a fairly well connected narrative, still it will be helpful here to outline the cruise and to supplement the accounts of certain episodes. Because many geographical names in this region were often arbitrarily assigned by self-confident occidental explorers, and many have since been changed, it has been necessary to identify places mentioned in these dispatches by reference to charts of Perry's expedition[13] and to the large charts from the Ringgold-Rodgers squadron which recently have been transferred from the Navy's Hydrographic Office to the Division of Maps and Charts in The National Archives. It is interesting to find these Americans of nearly a century ago exploring islands, such as Ōkinawa and Ie, which figured so prominently in the final stages of the recent war.

Lieutenant H. K. Stevens in the *Hancock* continued charting the eastern coast of Formosa before proceeding to Naha and from there to the Montgomery Islands slightly to the northwest. Acting Lieutenant William Gibson took the *Cooper* further to investigate the Amakirima group to the southwest of Great Liu Ch'iu. On April 27th the squadron cleared Naha harbor. The *Fenimore Cooper* left its companions and proceeded to locate rocks and to chart insular shores in the direction of Kyūshū. Bearing westward of that large island, the schooner's crew surveyed the Gotō Islands and others extending up to the island of Iki. Thus a succession of major channels was investigated. The Americans passed Hirado, the island on which the Dutch, English, and Portuguese had traded early in the seventeenth century before the Japanese Edict of Exclusion. On sailed the little craft through the Tsushima Strait (Krusenstern's) which separates Kyūshū and Honshū from Tsushima and Korea. Her scientists marked locations along the abrupt western coast of Nippon and were able to correct the maps of von

[13] *Narrative of the Expedition of An American Squadron to the China Seas and Japan . . . Under the Command of Commodore M. C. Perry . . .*, vol. II, Washington, A. O. P. Nicholson, 1856, map appendices, espec. one entitled "Chart of the Coast of China and of the Japan Islands . . . by Lieuts. W. L. Maury and S. Bent. . . , 1855."

Siebold and Raper. They scouted around the Ōki Islands, the Nōtō Peninsula, and the island of Sadō. They passed through the Strait of Sangar (Tsūgarū) and on June 6th rejoined the squadron at Hakodaté.[14]

Meanwhile the *Hancock* and *Vincennes* had pushed northward to Ōshima, one island of several with this name, which lies nearly halfway between Great Liu Ch'iu and the southern tip of Kyūshū. After completing surveys of its perimeter and magnificent bay, they struck out for the treaty-port of Shimoda, skirting on the way the capes of Shikōku, and both arriving on May 13th.

Rodgers' negotiations with the Governors of Shimoda were conducted through the interpreter, Hōri Tatsunosuké, who was studying English with the aid of a Noah Webster dictionary donated by the Perry expedition. The right to travel on land was insisted upon; when naval men and officers found themselves hampered in their walks, they sometimes turned roughly on their guards. By request a bazaar such as Perry's crews had patronized was opened; the Americans were surprised to see prices marked in Arabic figures. Lieutenant Alexander W. Habersham noticed the relatively low value of gold and discerned an opportunity for speculation— a differential which later foreign exporters of the metal were to utilize. He and his associates believed that the Japanese had signed a treaty only to avoid hostilities and that it would require a "good filibusters' drubbing" to induce them to observe it in good faith. He was aware of a Japanese profit of two hundred per cent on transactions, indicating that one dollar still passed for approximately 1,600 cash, as had been the exchange rate during Perry's visits.[15]

Although the Governors of Shimoda refused to sanction a visit of the *John Hancock* to nearby Heda, she nevertheless

[14] For the charted route of this voyage, see a chart-map entitled "West Coast of Nippon, Northern Part," in the Division of Maps and Charts, The National Archives.

[15] *The North Pacific Surveying and Exploring Expedition*, Philadelphia, J. B. Lippincott & Co., 1857, pp. 236, 221-223, 202, 210-214, 228-229.

sailed for that port, charting the coast around Cape Idzū and into Sūruga Bay. Not long previously a Russian frigate, the *Diana*, had been spun by a tidal wave and had foundered. Her crew had sought refuge in Heda from the British and French, with whom their country was at war. Soundings proved that harbor to be superior to Shimoda, and the *Hancock's* crew returned to the treaty-port with criticism of Commodore Perry's judgment.

So fog- and rockbound is much of the coast from Edo Bay northeastward that Commander Rodgers favored sending a launch to trace the shore at close range. He was referred to Edo (or Yedo, present Tōkyō), the shogunal capital, for authority to execute this venture and to carry on the operations of the larger vessels around Ezo. This time Rodgers was prepared with a more remarkable letter to the "Honourable Secretary of State of the Empire of Japan." It had been translated into Dutch and Chinese. Nevertheless, the two warships left Shimoda toward the end of May without official permission, leaving the *Vincennes Junior* to chart 450 miles of rugged coastline.[16]

One of the most daring exploits in the annals of naval exploration was the voyage of these fifteen men in an open craft. Lieutenant Brooke, who commanded them, put his famous sounding lead to effective use. Edward M. Kern, an artist who had accompanied Frémont on one of his expeditions, went along to draw contours and to sketch the topography. By repeatedly camping on shore the Americans strained the interpretation of the provision in Perry's treaty which permitted vessels in emergency to find haven in non-treaty-ports. The *Vincennes Junior* reached Hakodaté safely in early June with exciting stories and valuable information.

During the next three weeks the crews busied themselves surveying, and with purchasing coal, foodstuffs, and souve-

[16] For the launch's route, see the chart-map entitled "East Coast of Nippon, Empire of Japan, Shimoda to Hakodadi," in the Division of Maps and Charts, The National Archives.

[14]

nirs. Both at Shimoda and Hakodaté Commander Rodgers became unexpectedly involved with the governors over the problems of American residence and trade under the Treaty of Kanagawa. Indeed, only fifteen days after Perry's final departure from Shimoda, the *Lady Pierce*, a clipper from the Golden Gate, owned by Silas E. Burrows, had appeared in Edo Bay with presents for shogunal officials and bringing one or two Japanese who had been rescued at sea. Her Captain Burr had been turned back to Shimoda. Subsequently, on March 15, 1855, a fortnight before treaty rights could be fully invoked at Shimoda, the *Caroline E. Foote* anchored there. She had been chartered by William C. Reed and T. T. Dougherty at Honolulu with the encouragement of the American commissioner and consul.[17] Clearing on February 13th, she had sailed with a cargo of ships' chandlery to supply forty whalers whose captains expected to outfit at Hakodaté in the following season.

Shortly after her arrival, the *Caroline E. Foote* had been chartered by the stranded Russians for the first of two contemplated voyages to safety at Petropavlovsk. Dougherty had accompanied Captain A. J. Worth on this trip, while application for residence on shore had been successfully made for Mr. and Mrs. W. C. Reed and their two children, Mr. and Mrs. H. H. Doty, Mrs. Worth, and Messrs. Edward A. Edgerton, William E. Bidleman, and Horace W. Peabody. The Japanese had been as curious to see the alien women and children as they were reluctant to receive them on shore. These self-styled "American pioneers in Japan" were housed in two temples near Shimoda in the village of Kakizaki, where later Townsend Harris, the first American consul-general to Japan, came to reside in August 1856.

When the *Vincennes* and *Hancock* arrived at Shimoda on May 13th, protests concerning restrictions and an official Japanese order to depart as soon as possible were lodged with Rodgers. All he could do here and at Hakodaté was to lec-

---

[17] David L. Gregg and D. A. Ogden, respectively.

ture the governors on the sanctity of treaties and to proclaim the aggressive doctrine that when "a treaty gives a thing, it gives every thing which is necessary to the enjoyment of the thing given." Furthermore, he warned and even threatened concerning the serious consequences which could result from American unfriendliness. He promised to provide his government with the correspondence of the controversy; the matter actually was referred to the new Commodore of the East India Squadron, Joel Abbott, and to the Navy Department.

Not until the squadron's appearance at Shimoda was Reed able to secure on credit a cargo of rice, silks, lacquer ware, and assorted novelties valued at $15,000. The American civilians immediately became overbearing and threatened their unwilling hosts with naval reprisals and even with an expedition of filibusters from California. When the *Caroline E. Foote* returned to Shimoda in the third week of May, she did not transport the second group of Russians to Siberia for fear of capture by a British man-of-war. Instead she was loaded for Hakodaté, whither Commander Rodgers agreed to deliver in advance Reed's and Dougherty's request for the privileges of residence, trade, and rental of a warehouse for the chandlery.

While Rodgers was anxious to secure residence ashore for merchants, he was embarrassed and irritated by two other alleged Americans who arrived on the clipper brig *Leveret*, having cleared from Honolulu in March of that year. This pair came to establish a grogshop for visiting seamen, but when refused a permit, they began to sell to sailors of the squadron. Rodgers forced them to leave on the *Caroline E. Foote* which, on June 27th, sailed for San Francisco via Shimoda and Guam.

Upon returning to California, Bidleman and Doty filed in a United States district court a protest under Articles IV and V of the Treaty of Kanagawa. The partners Reed and Dougherty complained of their loss in a memorandum addressed to Secretary of State William L. Marcy. In these statements and in reports to the press these disgruntled merchants were in substantial agreement with Rodgers' dispatches to Secretary Dobbin. In their opinion the Japanese should not only be compelled by naval demonstrations to fulfill the agreements already concluded, but a new commercial treaty should be negotiated, with naval pressure if necessary. It would be more effective if this instrument could be signed at Edo and its commercial provisions published throughout the empire. It should stipulate a more equitable ratio of currency exchange and permit individual transactions between American and Japanese merchants. Consular agents should be admitted at treaty-ports and better harbors should be opened for trade. Finally, it was proposed that a respectable squadron should patrol Japanese waters until such a commercial agreement could be tested. Most of these suggestions were carried out by Townsend Harris and the United States Navy during the ensuing four years.

But the government in Washington did not join in the fulminations of journals like the *San Francisco Daily Herald* which denounced the "perfidious Japanese," declaring that in espousing the cause of American merchants the government might more appropriately bombard several towns than conciliate differences. And James Gordon Bennett's *New York Herald* issued a blast under the headlines:

VERY IMPORTANT FROM JAPAN.

THE TREATY WITH THE UNITED STATES REPUDIATED
BY THE JAPANESE.

AMERICANS NOT ALLOWED TO RESIDE AT THE THREE PORTS.

TREATIES MADE BY JAPAN WITH RUSSIA, FRANCE AND ENGLAND.

WHAT WILL THE ADMINISTRATION DO?[18]

[18] *San Francisco Daily Herald*, September 18, 1855. *The New York Herald*, October 15, 1855. A Russo-Japanese treaty, signed in February 1855, had opened to Russian merchantmen not only Shimoda and Hakodaté but also Nagasaki, where the Dutch had traded. By the most-favored-nation clause in the Treaty of Kanagawa, access to Nagasaki likewise and automatically became available to American vessels.

The expedition's commanders must have felt a certain relief in putting to sea from Hakodaté on June 28-29, 1855. The *Vincennes* ran along the Kuriles to Petropavlovsk, skirted the coast of Siberia to Bering Strait, and there left a boat's crew with Lieutenant Brooke and artist Kern for astronomical and other observations. Then the flagship pushed into the Arctic Ocean to Herald Island and as far north as 72° 05′ in a vain search for Wrangel's Land. After making soundings of particular value to whalers, she returned to pick up the party in Bering Strait and proceed with deep-sea soundings off the Aleutians on her way to San Francisco, which was reached on October 13th. The *Fenimore Cooper* had arrived at the rendezvous two days earlier, having charted longer in the Aleutians in search of coal and news of the shipwrecked whaler *Monongahela*.

The *John Hancock* completed her charting of the Strait of Sangar and of the northern shores of Honshū; then Lieutenant Stevens steered up the western coast of Ezo and through La Perouse (Soya) Strait. Next he scouted along western Sakhalin, recorded the northern approach to the Amur River, and charted the northern coast of the Sea of Okhotsk and the western coast of Kamchatka. A special search for coal in this area had been ordered, but only an inferior mine in the northwestern portion of the Kamchatka Peninsula was discovered. In September the steamer terminated surveying along Siberian shores and was the last to reach San Francisco (October 19th). In addition to their negative results, these voyages provided important information about the Great Circle route between American ports and the emporia of Eastern Asia.

All of the expedition's officers realized that much work remained to be done in regions they had visited. Stevens regretted that whalers still were inadequately protected off northern Ezo, the Kuriles, and Sakhalin. Rodgers expressed to Secretary Dobbin the wish that three oceanic belts between San Francisco and Shanghai could be surveyed in preparation for vastly expanded trans-Pacific trade by steam and sail.

But appropriations were more than exhausted, so the *Vincennes* stood out of the Golden Gate on February 2, 1856, and after surveys in the Sandwich and Society Islands in March and April, Rodgers took her around the Horn and made the Brooklyn Navy Yard by mid-July. The *Fenimore Cooper* was placed in ordinary at Mare Island, while the *John Hancock* was dispatched to help pacify Indians in the Northwest.

Although our correspondence ends at San Francisco, some of the expedition's scientists were not through with their labors. Ringgold had returned to active work in Washington on the charts and other records of the squadron. Lieutenants Silas Bent and W. L. Maury had been assigned from Perry's mission for similar studies at the National Observatory, where a "Japan Expedition Office" was established. They were soon joined by Rodgers, John M. Brooke, and William Gibson. Although three large volumes were published to register the historic and scientific achievements of the Japan Expedition, no comparable work on the Surveying Expedition to the North Pacific Ocean ever appeared. Editing and compilation were still in progress when Fort Sumter spoke Civil War. Rodgers' contributions did not end until 1866.[19]

Before war swept Lieutenant John Brooke into an infant Confederate States Navy, he rendered another service to the Union. On April 9, 1858, he was ordered to plan and command a surveying cruise for the charting of proposed steamship routes between California and China. In Washington Brooke had met Joseph Hikōzō, a Japanese youth who had been rescued from a disabled junk and had received an education and baptism in the United States. With Hikōzō as captain's clerk, Brooke assumed command of the *Fenimore Cooper*, still at Mare Island, and on September 26th they sailed. For forty-three days they sounded along the most frequented routes toward the Sandwich Islands and China, recording fewer shoals and dangers than existing charts indi-

[19] U.S. Navy Department, *Report of the Secretary of the Navy for 1860*, pp. 18, 48.

cated. From December 29th to February 7th (1859), when the expedition returned to Honolulu, surveys and corrections were made around the reefs and islands northwest of the Hawaiian Kingdom. Hikōzō was released at Honolulu for a direct passage to Hongkong, his place being filled by another Japanese known as "Tim" by the sailors. On March 9th the *Fenimore Cooper* stood southwestward on an irregular course taking her to the Ladrones (Marianas) and other islands which were important for guano, for whalers, or as depots or hazards for the projected trans-Pacific line. Hongkong harbor was entered on May 19th.

Brooke then took the *Cooper* northward to the Liu Ch'iu Islands and reached Yokohama on August 13th. Ten days later, the schooner was wrecked in a cyclone, but her crew, instruments, and records were saved. Provisions on shore were made for the stranded expedition, and in February 1860, Lieutenant Brooke took passage as naval advisor on the *Kanrin Maru*, the first Japanese steamer to venture across the Pacific.[20]

Such is the background of this important Surveying Expedition to the North Pacific Ocean. From now on let the officers give their own accounts.

ALLAN B. COLE
Pomona College and
The Claremont Graduate School

[20] On the Brooke expedition, see a memorandum in the Office of Naval Records and Library, The National Archives; *U. S. Sen. Ex. Doc. No. 2*, Serial No. 1025, 36th Cong., 1st Sess., pp. 1150-1151. Also see Joseph Heco, *The Narrative of a Japanese*, edited by James Murdoch, I, pp. 157-158, 172-184, 238-239; Yokohama, Yokohama Printing and Publishing Co., Ltd., 1894. See also *National Intelligencer*, September 9, 1859. Before World War II, the *Monumenta Nipponica Monograph Series* had contracted to publish Lieutenant Brooke's journal.

The editor of this volume takes this opportunity to thank staff members of the Office of Naval Records and Library, Navy Department, and of The National Archives, especially in the Division of Maps and Charts, for efficient assistance.

In the letters which follow, the punctuation has been modified slightly for ease of reading, but care has been taken not to change the original meaning. The original spellings have been retained.

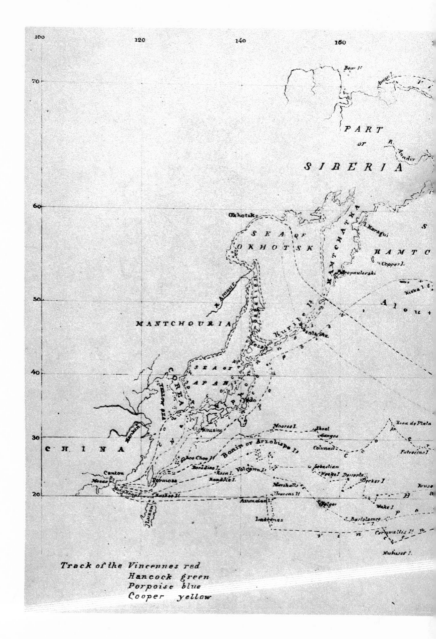

Track of the Vincennes red
        Hancock green
        Porpoise blue
        Cooper yellow

Map bound with

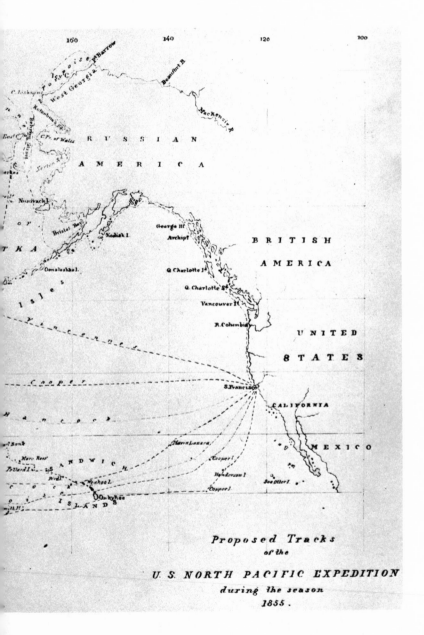

Proposed Tracks

of the

U. S. NORTH PACIFIC EXPEDITION

during the season

1855.

ters of the expedition

Map bound with the letters of the expedition.

Letters of the Surveying Expedition
to Japan and the North Pacific Ocean
1853-1856

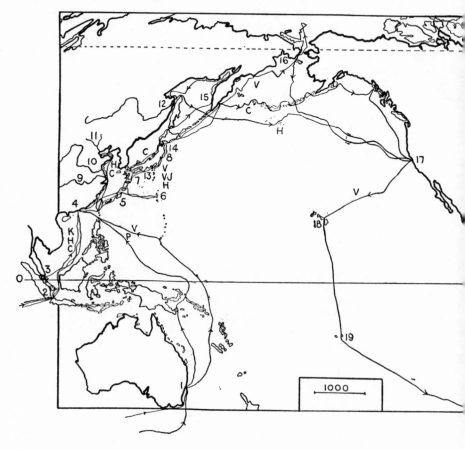

Actual Routes Sailed by Vessels of the Expedition

INITIAL LETTERS OF SHIPS:

Vincennes (V)
Launch *Vincennes Junior* (VJ)
John Hancock (H)
Porpoise (P)
John P. Kennedy (K)

NUMBERED LOCATIONS:

1. Sydney, Australia
2. Sunda Strait
3. Singapore
4. Hongkong-Canton area
5. Okinawa (Great Liu Ch'iu)
6. Bonin (Ogasawara) Is-lands, including Peel Is-land and Port Lloyd
7. Island of Kyūshū
8. Main Island of Honshu
9. Yangtze River
10. Huang (Yellow River)
11. Pei Ho (North River)
12. Mouth of Amur River
13. Treaty Port of Shimoda
14. Treaty Port of Hakodaté
15. Petropavlovsk on Kam-chatka Peninsula
16. Leniavine Strait, where landing party stayed
17. San Francisco
18. Kingdom of Hawaii
19. Tahiti

Letters &c from Commander JOHN RODGERS
Commanding Surveying Expedition
to North Pacific Ocean, Behring's Straits
and China Seas

U.S. Ship Vincennes
Hong-Kong

[Secretary of the Navy James C. Dobbin]   August, 1854

Sir:

In consequence of the illness of Captain [Cadwalader] Ringgold and his condemnation by a board of medical officers, the command of the Surveying Expedition, which had been entrusted to him, has devolved upon myself.

From causes various in their nature and which it would not be interesting for me to relate, many changes had become necessary. While I am abundantly able, I think, to show full cause for the somewhat sweeping hand with which I have carried out these changes, I hope that I may be spared the pain of narrating them, since I flatter myself, no complaint will be made of my action from the gentleman concerned.

The Store Ship John P. Kennedy, even after the extensive repairs put upon her by order of Captain Ringgold, remains too much decayed for general sea service—still less fit is she for the peculiarly exposed duty to which surveying vessels are liable. To have repaired the Kennedy fully would have cost no less perhaps than to build a new vessel, while the hull, when finished, would have been patch-work. . . .

Coming as I did into a command which had fallen into a state of disorganization, my position has been one of trial and difficulty. Very fortunately I have been able in many things to throw myself upon the experience, judgement and good offices of Commodore Perry, who has been most kind to me. The difficulties have principally been vanquished and the future seems bright. I have every thing to hope from the zeal and intelligence of the officers who are to cooperate with me. The work to be done is plain, and the rest is easy.

[23]

I deem that the field of the work of the American Surveying Expedition lies principally in the North Pacific Ocean
and its bays and inlets. The route between Australia and the
British possessions in the East is more particularly a British
interest. No one but ourselves has any desire to survey the
particular fields of our commercial enterprise. Our ships from
San Francisco to China and our Whalers in the Pacific, and
waters which empty into it, whiten the Ocean. For them, if I
judge rightly, was this expedition fitted out.

While the field then, which I think allotted to me, is
broad, it is also well defined; and nothing unknown which I
can take up in this vast theatre is without value and significance to our commercial career. . . .

The plan which I have selected is the one which upon
mature consideration appears to offer the greatest results.
While it seems bold, I think it will escape the imputation of
rashness. The season at present is too advanced for us to penetrate far North. We shall however find employment in surveying islands in temperate regions, until the middle of next
February. We shall then return to this place [Hongkong],
fill up with provisions and repair the vessels. I propose then
to start about the first day of March, to carry out the work
sketched on the accompanying piece of tracing paper, giving
to each vessel the portion which is there alloted to her. The
plan is large enough to embrace two seasons. Full justice can
scarcely be done to it in one; much however can certainly be
accomplished, but I may have to leave to some more fortunate
man the honor of perfecting what we have drawn hastily.

It is reasonable to suppose that you have a solicitude to
know whet[h]er this opportunity has fallen into fit hands. I
therefore beg leave to refer to a few friends who, I flatter
myself, will express the belief that I am not unworthy of
trial. Having been for some time on the Coast Survey, I beg
leave to refer to Professor [Alexander D.] Bache for his
opinions as to my surveying skill. While Professor [Jean L.
R.] Agassiz knows that I have little acquaintance with the

Natural sciences, I am persuaded, he is assured, that I am not without interest in them. Lt. Charles Davis, Superintendent of the Nautical almanac, will add his testimony that I am not absolutely unfit to make or direct the requisite observations of the heavenly bodies, and I believe that Lt. [Matthew F.] Maury will think I am able to comprehend the subjects to be effected. An assumption of good temper and of ability to deal with men may be made perhaps from the fact that I commanded during the Florida war successively the "Schooner Wave" and the Brig "Jefferson" for a period of nearly three years. For a like time I commanded the "Petrel," the "Hetzel" and then the "Legare" on the Coast survey and the "John Hancock" for a year and a half in this expedition. While I have never had serious difficulty with officer or man under my command, nor troubled the Department with courts, nor complaints, I have always I believe preserved a proper measure of discipline and good order.

Of this I am quite sure: I shall not fail because I want interest in the things which have fallen to me. I have the honor to be, Sir

Your obedient servant,
JOHN RODGERS
Lt. Commanding U.S. Surveying
Expedition to the North Pacific Ocean

Honorable James C. Dobbin
Secretary of the Navy of the
United States
Washington, D.C.

U.S. Ship Vincennes
Hong-Kong
September 8th, 1854

[Secretary Dobbin]
Sir:

I have the honor to report that we sail tomorrow for the prosecution of our duties. . . .

The temper of the officers and crews is excellent. Of their abilities no doubt has been expressed.

I have the honor to enclose a letter of instructions to Lt. Commanding H. K. Stevens, a copy of which was sent to Acting Lieutenant Commdg. Wm. Gibson of the Schooner "Fenimore Cooper" for his guidance in case of separation.

With this vessel and the "Porpoise" we proceed first to the Bonin [Ōgasawara] Islands, and then to the Ladrones [Marianas], so as to escape in some degree the risk of Ty-foons, so probable at this season and so dangerous to a vessel surveying in confined waters with no known port at hand. To these Islands particular attention has been drawn by the instructions to Captain Ringgold from the Department. About the middle of November we shall close in with the coast of Japan and make some examinations of the Islands adjacent to it. Much has already been done by Commodore Perry to survey these islands and the Bonin Group. By the first or tenth of February we shall return to this port, and before the first of March I hope to leave here on my way to Behring's Straits, surveying the coasts, bays, harbors and islands on the Asiatic shores, advancing continually to the North, as the weather grows warmer. At Petropaulowski I propose to establish an observatory, upon permission obtained from the proper authorities and thence to send the "Porpoise" to survey the Aleoutian Group and the coast of America to the North through Behring's straits, as far as the circumstances will permit. In the "Vincennes" I shall keep on the Asiatic shore, as less known.

In St. Lawrence Bay at the entrance of Behring's straits I may leave an officer with a guard, should circumstances warrant it, to make observations there for absolute longitude and upon magnetic declination ectr.

The detail of the vessels for the proposed survey to commence next February from here was sent to you by last mail.

Early in November 1855 it is proposed that, having finished our work for the whaling interest, all the vessels shall rendezvous in San Francisco, when we shall as soon as possible commence the survey of the route between California and China and the impediments to navigation in it.

The voyage across the Pacific to Hong-Kong will occupy some six months, as we shall endeavour to fill up the time for which the provisions will last in making as thorough a survey as possible. When we arrive in Hong-Kong about April or May 1856, I trust we shall have completed our labors.

I have the honor to be

    very respectfully

       Your obedient servant,

               JOHN RODGERS
               Lt. Commdg. U.S. Surveying
Honourable James C. Dobbin   Expn. to the North Pacific Ocean
Secretary of the U.S. Navy
Washington, D.C.

There follows a letter from Commander Rodgers to Lieutenant H. K. Stevens, dated September 6, 1854, in which Stevens is instructed to take the steamer *John Hancock*, towing the schooner *Fenimore Cooper*, to Shanghai, there to meet Robert McLane, American Commissioner to China, and his Secretary of the Legation, Dr. Peter Parker.

If Messrs. McLane and Parker desired to go northward to the mouth of the Peiho for negotiations with Chinese authorities, Stevens was to convey them. He was to take this opportunity for cursory surveying of places in the Yellow Sea and in bays and river mouths adjacent to it. Especially was he to examine the mouth of the Yellow River and to search for good harbors on the western coast of Korea.

The two vessels on their return voyage were to reach Formosa via Shanghai and were to survey the eastern coast of that island. At Keelung [Ch'i Lung] in northern Formosa the rest of the expedition might be met.

A sixteen-page report on botanical specimens is here omitted. These specimens were forwarded from the expedition to the Navy Department in September of 1854.

Also omitted are the itemized contents of a box of charts and journals which had been drawn and written under the supervision of

Commander Cadwalader Ringgold, the flag officer who preceded Rodgers. This collection was destined for the Bureau of Ordnance and Hydrography.

U.S. Ship Vincennes
Hong-Kong
September 8th, 1854

[Secretary Dobbin]

Sir:

There is reason to believe that coal may be found in the Aleutian Islands.

It is a somewhat delicate matter to judge whet[h]er prudence would dictate making the examination before permission shall be obtained from the Russians or afterwards. I beg leave respectfully to request instructions to be sent to Hong-Kong in regard to this point, to meet me here by the first of February next, should the Department deem the question of moment.

From a conversation which I had with Lieutenant Maury, Superintendent of the National Observatory, before leaving the United States, I shall be inclined, should no instructions reach me, first to ask permission, as better furthering our views.

I have the honor to be
very respectfully
Your obedient servant,

JOHN RODGERS
Lt. Commdg. U.S. Surveying
Honorable James C. Dobbin   Expn. to the North Pacific Ocean
Secretary of the U.S. Navy
Washington, D.C.

A letter, dated December 1, 1854, from Acting Lieutenant William Gibson of the *Fenimore Cooper* to Lieutenant Henry K. Stevens describes the former's observations during the recent voyage up the China coast to Shanghai and then from Shanghai into the Gulf of Pechihli with Messrs. McLane and Parker on board. They had sailed up the Peiho in the direction of Tientsin, ignoring the remonstrances of local mandarins, but, meeting a boom of boats strung across the river, they later dropped down stream. They had sighted part of the Shantung Peninsula. Wherever they had gone they had sketched shorelands and had taken samples of sea bottom. Also they had observed tides and river mouths.

In the following letter the more interesting paragraphs will be quoted, the rest being abstracted. Commander Rodgers reported that the brig *Porpoise* was overdue and had failed to meet rendezvous either at Port Lloyd in the Bonin Islands [Ōgasawara-shima] or at Naha, the chief port of Great Liu Ch'iu Island, now more commonly called Okinawa. The commander of the *Porpoise* had been Acting Lieutenant William King Bridge.

Rodgers went on to describe how the *Vincennes* had recently completed a cruise on which her crew had surveyed Rosario and Borodino Islands, between the Liu Ch'ius and Bonins. Continuing eastward they had reconnoitered in the Coffin Islands, a southward extension of the Bonins, and had turned north to chart Port Lloyd. Moreover, twenty-two islands west of the Liu Ch'ius had been plotted, and it had been found that the island of Ykima, which was placed on most charts to the south of the Maikoshima group, had no existence at all. Then we come to interesting information about relations with the Liu Ch'iuan natives.

U.S. Ship Vincennes
At sea

[Secretary Dobbin]   December 17th, 1854

Sir:

... The Government of Loo-Choo appears inveterably opposed to foreign intercourse and seeks to delay on every occasion and by frivolous pretenses the assistance to ships, which by convention with Commodore Perry it is bound to render. The want of energy incident to their insular position and to their long seclusion from intercourse with more enterprising nations would I think in part be palliated by the presence of a consul, who would during his residence amongst them find avenues for the prompt despatch of business, which are closed to strangers. The people do not seem averse to foreign intercourse. If the geographical position of Loo-Choo and Japan should appear to make them desirable stopping places to our vessels, no means so apt could be devised to render nugatory their jealous fears as such an appointment. Until the temper of these Governments has changed, we cannot hope for commerce with them. The seclusion of ages is deeply marked in their foreign policy. They will give nothing and take nothing which can be avoided. An agent on the spot to report delinquencies and gradually to overcome their reluctance appears both the cheapest and the kindest way in which it can be done.

The American clipper ship "What Cheer," Captn. Baker from Hong-Kong bound to California, put in to Loo-Choo in October last in want of provisions and water. The Government reported to me that Captn. Baker had been furnished with these articles to the amount of One Hundred and Fifty Seven 60/100 Dollars, that Captn. Baker paid Seventy Five Dollars on this account and sailed leaving the balance of Eighty Two 60/100 Dollars unpaid. The amount due I caused to be refunded and will forward the report of the Loo-Choo Government of the facts upon my arrival in Hong-Kong, with a translation by Dr. Parker.

This sum was not important, but the Loo-Chooans are defenseless themselves, and with no consul to take cognizance of the acts of foreign vessels, they are liable to gross outrages. The Loo-Choo Government in reporting this act of Captn. Baker did so with an amiable reluctance and strenuously hoped that his Excellency the President of the United States would not cause him to be beheaded, nor even bambooed. . . .

The *John Hancock* under Lieutenant Stevens and the *Fenimore Cooper* under Acting Lieutenant Gibson returned to Hongkong from Shanghai, North China, and Formosa on February 13, 1855. In a letter, written from Shanghai on January 21st, Stevens described for Rodgers the operations of the two vessels since the previous September 9th, when they had left Hongkong for Shanghai and the north.

A following letter, Stevens to Rodgers, was written at Hongkong on February 13th (after rejoining the flagship). In it Stevens told of having left Shanghai on January 28th and of having proceeded to Keelung on Formosa by way of the Chinese port of Wênchow.

[30]

On the day after arriving at Hongkong (February 14th) Acting
Lieutenant Gibson reported to Rodgers on the *Fenimore Cooper's*
voyage southward from Shanghai. To Stevens' account he added
data concerning weather conditions, coastal features, and inland
topography and productivity of Formosa.

U.S. Ship Vincennes
Hong-Kong

[Secretary Dobbin]   February 15th, 1855.

Sir!

I purposely refrain from giving you hydrographic details
by this mail, as our results are not quite finished, but by the
next one on the first of March I propose to send charts, astronomical observations, and remarks on such of our peculiar
duties as we have been able to effect.

I shall confine myself in this letter to observations upon
the islands, & upon our intercourse with the people whom we
have met.

We reached the Bonin Islands on the 19th of October
1854. It rather appears to me that the Bonin Islands are not
very important to our commerce. I think they will be found
to lie inside of the ellipse formed by the tracks of our vessels
in the trade between China and our Pacific States. This point,
however, Lieut. Maury of the Observatory is much better
calculated to discuss than I can pretend to be.

The inhabitants of Peel Island are 30 in number, of these
8 are white, and 22 Sandwich Islanders [Hawaiians].

It is mountainous and very healthy, the greater part of it
is not arable, the valleys are fertile, and produce immense
crops of sweet potatoes, which are the staple of the island.
Green turtle come in large numbers to the shores to breed.
About a thousand of them, weighing 300 pounds each, are
taken annually for the wants of the inhabitants, part of them
salted, and the rest kept in pens built on salt water for consumption in the island or sale to casual vessels. The wants
and habits of the people are simple, they are satisfied with

sweet potatoes, turtle, and rum obtained from whalers for turtle and sweet potatoes.

From the Bonins we proceeded on a cruise in their vicinity, [and] on the 16th of November [we] arrived in the Loo-Choo [Islands].

The physical peculiarities of the Loo-Chooans have been so gracefully depicted by Bazil Hall[21] that nothing interesting can be said about them now.

Finding after my arrival that the authorities were inclined to take little notice of the Vincennes, and that the civility on their part was confined to sending to me a few provisions with the card of the Governor of Napa, I requested an audience with the Regent. It was granted, and held in the court-house of Napa.

As many of us as could be spared from the duties of the vessel attended, accompanied by nearly the whole guard of marines.

The Revd. Mr. G. F. Moreton, English Episcopal Missionary to Loo-Choo kindly consented to be the interpreter and I made the following address to His Highness the regent.

1. "That I and the officers were grateful to him for the honour he had conferred in suffering us to pay our respects;

2. "That it was gratifying to my government to have one more nation added by the convention with Commodore Perry to the honourable list of its respected friends;

3. "That I had been annoyed at hearing a merchant-vessel, the 'What Cheer,' had gone off without paying for supplies, that I hoped he would bring it officially before me, in order that the facts might be reported to my government;

4. "That I was very sorry a pilot had not been sent out to me. The neglect was an infringment on their part of a convention. It was a law of Europe and America that treaties broken on one side invite aggression on the other;

[21] Basil Hall was a captain in the British Royal Navy. In 1818 he had published a work entitled *Account of a Voyage of Discovery to the West Coast of Corea and the Great Loo-Choo Islands.*

5. "That I regretted the buoys placed on the shoals by Commodore Perry had been suffered to go adrift; that the safety of vessels is now, after our treaty, an object of moment to the Loo-Chooans; that buoys might possibly serve to guide vessels when pilots would not go out;

6. "That I should feel extremely honoured at having the company of His Highness the regent on board."

Those sentences I read one by one from a paper in my hand to Mr. Moreton, who translated them into Loo Choo to I-cher-a-chi-chi, the government interpreter,[22] who went to the chair of the regent and repeated them into his ear with a low voice.

To this it was answered by the regent: 1. "that he was very glad to receive me and the officers of the Vincennes; 2. "that he was happy to be on good terms with the United States; 3. "that the affair of the 'What Cheer' was of little moment; that the Loo-Chooans had no use for money, and that he hoped I would not think seriously of the matter."

(The fact is that they had been exceedingly disturbed at the non-payment of their bills and had requested Mr. Moreton to represent the matter to the Commissioner to China, Mr. McLean [McLane]. Mr. Moreton had done so, and giving me upon our arrival his letter, which he had had no opportunity of sending, referred its contents to me for my action.) I replied that it was of moment that our people should be just, that it concerned the government to take cognizance of offences committed abroad. The regent finally said that he left the matter to myself; 4. "that the Loo-Chooans were bad sailors, and their boats were miserable; that they could not venture far from shore in rough weather without running the risk of being drowned."

I looked upon that as throwing the weight of acquiescence in their infringement of the convention in a material point upon myself, and I replied that what they had agreed to do was

[22] Chinese was the language used in these negotiations. Ichirazichi knew only a little English, but he was fluent in the dialect of Peking.

[33]

law; and the treaty must be carried out. That Commodore Perry had offered them a good boat which they had refused; that by treaty they had agreed to provide one themselves; and now it was time they had procured it. Their whole plea I looked upon as a manifest evasion.

5. The regent said "that the buoys had not been placed in their charge, and that a hurricane had driven them from their moorings; but that now they would have better buoys put down and kept in their places;

6. "That it was quite uncertain whether he should have it in his power to visit the Vincennes."

I had sent the evening before a copy to Mr. Moreton of what I have first put down as my remarks, in order that he might have a deliberate translation, and that the government interpreter might arrange their replies. A discussion took place occupying some minutes under each head.

We gained two points: we did not acquiesce in their not sending out pilots, and they consented to have the reefs properly and permanently buoyed. Our boats at their request put down buoys in such positions as I designated as a guide to themselves in placing better ones.

We found difficulties in procuring supplies. Our requests were met with constant evasions. At first they had desired that I would be content for the ships supplies with beef and pork alternately; that they were very poor people and needed their cattle for agriculture; I said, Yes, every other day would do. They did not supply the beef however. I sent a remonstrance; they repeated that they were very poor people, and could not supply beef every other day, but that they would do so twice a week. I said, "Well, twice a week would do." It was not supplied. After I heard of the wreck of the Wm. P. Sayward, I asked for a pilot to take us out, none was sent, and after waiting from morning to midday, I was forced to go without one. I had asked for an express to be sent to the wreck and to return with word whether she had sunk—none came.

We found the people ran away from us and their stalls

when we went into the markets; we could not buy anything except from the government. The supply of every egg was a government affair.

Now it is obvious that since people bring things to market to sell, that they would be glad to sell them to us if permitted to do so. It is as clear that the government forbids them to sell under penalties so heavy as to cause terror, even at the offer of buying.

The punishments of the Loo-Chooans are very cruel. Mr. Moreton the clergyman had one of his servants so severely treated as to be seriously injured for saying that he was a little unwell and would like a dose of medicine which was given. The asking for European medicine was a crime, reported by one of his fellow servants to the government. All his servants, Mr. Moreton says, are spies on him and one another, lest they should become attached to his family, they are changed every ten days or two weeks. Of course for people with manners so different it takes as much time to learn enough of European customs to become useful. Any consul should, I think, take his servants with him.

The punishment which the man in question had undergone consisted in having two pieces of heavy bamboo placed across the neck, and the ends brought together with cords; the bamboos were then by repeated efforts forced thus tied together down to his heels taking off his skin and violently disturbing the viscera. This is a minor punishment. Mr. Moreton was told this by the man himself who having been permitted to remain longer has become attached to him. The others are all government spies and this man as well, but he has become from circumstances a spy on the government rather than for it.

Wood and water were sent in insufficient quantities. Of water there is of course plenty, wood I really believe is scarce enough to make it dear; but we saw large piles, such as would serve an American woodmerchant for his stock. It was clear that the supply of wood on hand was abundant. They wished to know how many pounds of wood we wanted. When told they said they could not furnish so much. Finding that I was more pertinacious in requiring six cords to complete our quantity than I had been with other things, the government interpreter reported to Mr. Moreton for my information that "if they furnished the wood we demanded it would take every stick on the island, that none would be left for them to cook their food, that they would all die of starvation, and finally all Loo-Choo would become one vast sepulchre."

This very pretty figure of speech had less effect than they had hoped; first, because we had seen fifty times the quantity we required, cut, piled, and ready for sale; next, because the wood was necessary for the ship. Their making use of so bold a figure shows that they believed we were simple, credulous people, easily imposed upon, and very soft hearted.

I deemed a display of energy absolutely required; we had endured a long course of evasion, of subterfuge, of practical refusal to abide by the treaty. They had forced us at last to take a stand, and I was glad it should be upon wood rather than food. This I deemed the more important as I fancied it was an experiment upon our forebearance, a trial of how far they might practically evade their convention at only the expense of a few untruths. I believed that my acquiescence would be taken for a precedent, and their subterfuges were part of a systematic attempt to make the convention waste paper. I thought it important to show that we regarded it as law.

I replied that if the wood were not furnished in twenty-four hours, I should take an armed force with a field piece up to the palace, and learn from the regent why he infringed the convention of his government with the United States.

They apparently took me too for an oriental, and supposed I did not necessarily mean what I said.

The wood did not come, and I accordingly landed about 100 men, officers, sailors, and marines, all armed, & with one of Dahlgren's field pieces, marched up to the palace at Sheudi [Shui or Shuri][23].

They said the young king would die of fright at the sight of so many armed men. The reply was obvious; that it was to be hoped he would learn to make his mandarins observe the treaty. The heir apparent is said to be about 14 years old. Before we set out I-cher-a-chi-chi wished to know whether I would receive the regent on the beach, and have our conference there. I said no, I should do as I had threatened, go to the palace.

When in Sheudi they told me the regent was waiting to receive me at a house by the road side. We marched steadily on. They then said a feast was prepared for us; we still marched on. At last they requested that I would not take the men inside the walls running around the grounds of the palace; I readily said that I would not.

The people thronged the wayside, they filled all the cross streets in dense crouds. Their expression was however that of curiosity and pleasure. They took it for an honour, for a tributary offering possibly.

The clank of the wheels of the fieldpiece on the stone-pavement, and the tread of the men were the only noise.

Evidently they had calculated in our stopping by the way-side, for as I rejected the feast by saying that I had come to complain of their conduct, not to a feast, a number of men started at full speed toward the palace, and when we arrived there the gates were wide open. Two stone lions guarded the portal.

I entered, accompanied by some of the officers, leaving some of them in charge of the men.

They went in with pistols in their belts; I was unarmed. The grouping and stage effect were striking. I regarded the whole matter as a trial of skill. An Asiatic race had been trying to carry their point by Asiatic weapons; we were pleading the

[23] Commodore Perry had carried out an even greater military display in marching on the Liu Ch'iuan capital for similar reasons and objectives.

treaty, and endeavouring to show that we expected compliance with it. They had been using evasion, subterfuge, and all manners of disingenuousness to avoid giving us supplies, and so to induce us to leave, and never to come back again; to render their port worthless to passing ships. With arguments of a different kind we were trying to convert their harbor into a useful stopping place, and with our humble means to expound in the only way which could reach their conviction that the treaty was law, and insisted upon under a penalty.

I-cher-a-chi-chi said that the regent had gone about twenty miles into the country the evening before, and that he could not receive me; that the Pu-ching kwan next in rank to him would do so with the Tafung-kwan, governor of Napa.[24] He had just before said that the regent was waiting for me at a feast.

I did not appear to notice the discrepancy, but said that I wished to complain to the government, and I did not care whom it was said to if they would learn by it.

Chairs and tables were brought into the building, and the officers were all seated. Sacki, tea, and cakes were offered.

I had written a paper (enclosed and marked A) commenting upon their disingenuousness in language, which though deserved I found I had not the heart to use to timid and helpless old gentlemen. I contented myself with recapitulating the instances in which they had broken their engagements, that their whole conduct had been a course of evasion, that I was grieved that they had forced me to take other than a courteous manner toward them. That we wanted wood.

They replied that the inferiors were to blame, and that, if I wished it, they would punish them. I answered to this that I had nothing to do with the disobedience of inferiors, that I looked to them. The high officers evidently wished to make a peace-offering of innocent victims.

I finally said that it appeared they were unable to carry out

[24] The former official has been identified as a treasurer; the latter is called the "mayor" of Naha in the *Narrative* of the Perry Expedition.

in good faith what they agreed to do, that I should recommend my government to appoint a consul. At this both the Loo-Choo officers rose and bowed in a supplicating manner. "Loo Choo man no want a consul," said I-cher-a-chi-chi, and this closed the conference.

As we went out, chairs & tables were borne before by runners, who were disfurnishing the palace to furnish the house where we had been invited to accept a feast as we came up, and which invitation was now repeated.

They gave us an entertainment, and to the sailors and marines they gave tea. I presented to the Pu-ching kwan & Tafung-kwan each a carbine, with the hope that when they saw them, they would remember the treaty. We returned to the vessel about sunset.

Long strings of men were bringing down wood in their arms to the waterside all night, and at daylight the boats came alongside. About ten o'clock we had turned off two large junk loads of fuel; we had refused two bullocks and a quantity of other provisions; the bills were paid; a pilot was lying ahead of the vessel with an American flag in his boat on a long pole, ready to precede us; and we got underway.

On the 28th of Decbr. about sunset we anchored in Kago Sima Bay, off the town of Yamagawa.[25]

A large number of boats had collected near a neighbouring point; several came alongside. The people went below and examined everything. Their manners were polite. They showed eager curiosity.

After we had anchored, the boats dispersed. In the morning we rowed on shore to take observations. Some twenty men collected around, each with two swords [samurai], and motioned to us to go away. We went quietly on with our work. They came nearer, and we showed our revolvers to them as curiosities, explaining how they turned and how they took

[25] Kagōshima Bay is a deep indentation on the southern coast of the major Japanese island of Kyūshū. The town of Yamagawa is located on the western shore of the mouth of the bay or gulf.

apart. They were most struck with the Maynard primer, as resembling their own matches. We seemed unconscious of our display of force for we showed our arms with smiles.

The part which it became me to take was difficult to decide upon.

I presumed that they would interpret the treaty if they knew it to forbid our entering their ports except Simoda & Hakodadi, and that as landing on their shores had always before been forbidden, the magistrates might not feel authorized to permit it now.

We needed about ten thousand gallons of water to fill the vessel, and I said we wanted water. The supply was necessary since we could get it nowhere else so well. I determined to limit our positive demands to taking astronomical observations; and that in the meanwhile I would endeavour to get as much else as possible.

I said that it was desirable to go on the top of Mount Horner to observe. It was indeed a very important position. From its summit many islands to the Southward could be cut in. No answer was returned; I asked for an official interpreter; after a delay of some days a message was sent off to the effect that "no official interpreter was necessary."

I presume the interpreter could not know what to reply to me, and they therefore deemed it prudent to say nothing.

They brought off a rough drawing of a ship under all sail, and blew into the sails to intimate that we had better leave the harbor. I had offered to receive the governor or to call on shore, and pay my respects to him. No answer was returned to this. I did not think it politic to hold any personal communication with the petty authorities.

Finding that we were very much impeded in our attempts to take observations, I thought it prudent to define to the supreme government the position I had assumed for our conduct, and I accordingly wrote the enclosed letter marked B. to the "Hon. Secretary of State for foreign affairs, Empire of Japan." It did not appear necessary that such an officer should exist. The end was gained in bringing the letter under the eyes of [the] Japanese government, and it was believed the meaning of the direction would lead it into the proper hands.

I had a further view. The assertion of force would commit Europeans who could demand no less in making a survey, should we find after our arrival at Hong Kong the Expedition recalled. Without an expression of the kind, little hope I fear can be entertained of surveying in Japanese waters.

After the first day no one was permitted to go from the rock where the observations were taken. Our botanist was tantalized with what seemed to him new plants, just without his reach.

I deemed it of the last [first] importance to be very prudent. The authorities were responsible only to Jeddo.[26] As soon as we should pass the bounds they had mentally alotted to us, a collision must ensue. The local authorities would care nothing about foreign governments nor foreign relations.

The plea of humanity was also strong. Any mistake they might make in unknown duties by giving either too much or too little weight to our treaty, known probably only by rumour, must be expiated by suicide. Their path was full of uncertainty and danger. It would have been cruel to forget their position.

I had set limits to our own action, we would keep within them.

Finding that we gave way they determined probably to find whether we would assert any right whatever. Once when the boat was sent on shore to observe, as usual, a number of men

[26] Edo, or Yedo (modern Tōkyō), was at this time the seat of the *bakufu* (camp or military government) of Nippon, headed by the Shōgun. The highest shogunal council was called the Gō-Rōjū; foreign affairs was within the province of this body. There was no minister of foreign affairs.

In Commander Rodgers' later letters it will be seen that he shared with contemporary occidentals a misimpression according to which he referred to the Shōgun as the Emperor. Actually the Emperor had been reduced by the Tōkugawa Shōgun to ceremonial significance only. The imperial capital was located at Kyōtō, in central Japan.

with two swords came, and formed a cordon around her, while one more forward than the rest attempted to shove her off. The bowman who had laid in his oar, and taken his boat-hook as usual at landing, without any orders, struck the Japanese on the head. He partly slipped, and partly fell into the water. All his Japanese companions laughed loudly.

The boat came on board. I sent her back immediately, fully armed. The Japanese gave away. The quiet threat had carried our point, and we did not take arms ashore again.

Their policy changed. It was difficult to catch observations between the passing clouds. The Japanese now eagerly pointed out when the sun was about to appear between them.

I still said we wanted water. They asked whether we would go away when we received as much as we wanted. I gave no answer. By this time the observations were finished, and their patience exhausted. They sent the water; and we got underway. They would accept no payment for anything. Our only means of communication was by means of Medhurst's English & Chinese dictionary. The English words are not inflected, and we could not be sure that we selected in Chinese the meaning which we wished. Our manner of interchanging thoughts was neither commodious nor precise.

On the 9th of January we anchored in the roadstead at the Southern extremity of the island of Tanega Sima.[27]

Here the people were really kind. They asked by signs whether we needed wood or water. A few provisions were brought to the boats, unsolicited. We had landed with arms, as likely to prevent difficulty. The exhibition of force would obviate any necessary [sic] for using threats which are always irritating. They wished to prevent our leaving the beach. Finding that we were advancing however, they followed us. The climbing was severe, and in a little while the sailors had transferred their arms and instruments into the hands of the natives, and were walking by their sides.

[27] Tanegashima is a long, slim island (*shima*, or *jima*) just southeast of the mouth of the Bay of Kagōshima.

[42]

These people seemed scarcely to know the use of firearms. One of the officers caught the Japanese word for gun with which a very learned man was displaying his knowledge to his companions.

It strikes an American who from his childhood has seen children shoot, that ignorance of arms is an anomaly indicative of primitive innocence and Arcadian simplicity. We were unwilling to disturb it, and they did not learn from me that guns are fire-arms. They had brought down for the boats crew a handful of wood, a few vegetables, and a couple of chickens. I gave an embroidered silk pocket handkerchief for them to the man who brought them, and whose they seemed to be. This trading for foreign commodities could not be allowed, and after some five minutes deliberation the handkerchief was returned to me. The chief however could not resist its gaudy colours when offered to himself, and with a certain show of reluctance he accepted it.

On the 18th of January we anchored at Harbor, Bungalow, or Kikay Island, for it has been called by all these names.[28]

Here the people were more sophisticated than at Tanega Sima, and we held a conference as to whether we might ascend to the middle of the island to get observations. Nothing was concluded, and as it was important to secure the sun which only came out occasionally, we left them to deliberate alone, and marched off.

I was anxious to get ahead, and being unencumbered had outstripped the men who carried instruments. Looking back I saw a man on horseback with three spears as marks of his dignity borne by a man marching on foot, and accompanied by about a hundred people. They endeavoured to prevent our boats crew from following me. The sailors would advance a little and then would come a stoppage. There were also a few matchlock-men.

[28] Kikai Island lies about half way between Kyūshū and the Liu Ch'iu Islands. Together with its larger neighbor to the west, Ōshima (spelled Ousima by the Americans), Kikai is often mentioned in the dispatches.

The coxswain said one of them had drawn a knife upon him. I did not anticipate any difficulty in intimidating the gentleman who had probably thought we left the conference sooner than politeness warranted. I walked up to his horse, and shook my finger in his face with an appearance of anger, and then pulling out a very small revolver held it up to his view; I placed it so that he could look into all its chambers. He shuddered. It was a turn to the argument he had not looked for. Thus we carried out our wishes for peaceful observation.

We could not obtain enough provisions to make them a matter of moment. Just before we came to anchor a large herd of oxen were feeding in a meadow opposite to the vessel. As we approached the oxen were driven rapidly away. When we asked for beef, they said that they had no oxen. We could hear them lowing.

We had asked for enough provisions for several days consumption. A small pig was brought into an assembly of village magnates in their official robes, and with prostrations placed at their feet by the humbler Kikayans. A few bunches of turnips were next brought. With an air of timidity which they endeavoured to hide under an appearance of state they offered us them, and motioned us away. Having no object in staying, we went off to the vessel. No one could be induced to come on board. They had Japanese swords, matchlocks, and spears. They expressly asserted that they owed allegiance to Loo-Choo, and not to Japan.

On the 21st of January we anchored in the Bay of Sima-u, Island of Ousima. This bay is magnificent. Mountains rise out of blue water. The vegetation is stunted on the steep mountain sides, and it looks desolate. A few deserted patches of cultivation show where crops have not rewarded the agriculturist; the hills are covered with stunted trees, excellent apparently for fuel, and several cascades fall in silver threads from heights into the sea.

The village of Sima-u is composed of the most miserable population which I have ever seen. They were full of jealousy, however, lest we should see more of their land than was proper. With a companion I walked a few yards from the boat. A man ran before us and with a bow put his hands opposite to our breasts. I motioned, and said in as stern a tone as I could, "Go away." He repeated his bow, and advanced his hands closer to our breasts. I several times told him to go away; finding words of no avail, I presented a pistol from under my cloak. I do not think he quite comprehended me, for the instrument was nearly covered with cloth. Finding he did not understand I showed the weapon, more clearly. He ran away, and an older man came. To avoid further importunity, I made a circle, and shot into a large tree, and then put my finger upon the hole. They gave us no further trouble.

In all this repeated assertion of right to do innocent things, we took care never to be rude. The people are polite, simple, jealous, responsible to arbitrary superiors, and very timid. We were advancing the only reason for their acquiescence which would be listened to by those above them. Each of us did his duty. They in trying to obstruct us, we in not being stopped. Having this view of the matter we were never really ruffled, and the anger I sometimes appeared to feel was put-on for the occasion.

In the document marked C, which Mr. Parker has kindly consented to translate into Dutch and Chinese, I have used such arguments as could occur to me for granting permission to survey in Japan. I fear that they seem stronger to me than they will to the Japanese.

We are not war-vessels, and can not display much force, but I have come to the conclusion that the [United States] government would not be unwilling I should risk a collision with the Japanese in endeavouring to carry out our right. The trade is desirable, but the survey is a necessity. Under these circumstances it appears to me a "perfect right."

I shall bring temper, watchfulness, determination, and courtesy into the discussion. I hope to win, but I shall owe my success in a great degree to the firmness which I have concluded my government would wish me to show.

Circumstances have in the course of my duties, thrown me into positions involving discussions which wear something of a diplomatic character. With no higher authorities to consult I could only act as the emergencies of the case before me seem to demand.

I can have no dearer hope than that I may be judged to have done well.

The garrulousness of my letter will I trust be excused from its evident object. In wishing to tell everything of interest, I may easily have run into the extreme of saying too much.

I have the honour to be

very respectfully

Your obedient servant

JOHN RODGERS
Lt. Commanding U.S. Surveying
Expedition to the North Pacific Ocean

Honourable James C. Dobbin
Secretary of the United States
Navy
Washington, D.C.

Memorandum of remonstrance translated verbally to I-cher-a-chi-chi by the Revd. Mr. Moreton, but modified by me to the higher authorities in the palace at Sheudi in Loo-Choo.

That the whole conduct of the Loo-Choo Government has been marked by duplicity in not complying with their treaty stipulations.

I was told that Commodore Perry had made an agreement to receive fresh beef every other day. I agreed to every other day. It was not furnished. They said that it would ruin Loo Choo to give fresh beef oftener than once in four or five days. I agreed to this. The beef has not been furnished.

Pilots have never been sent. Excuses have been made that the weather was too bad when fishing boats were everywhere outside the reefs.

A messenger did not return from the wreck, as I desired, to let me know, whet[h]er she had sunk. After waiting many hours I was forced to leave without a pilot and without knowing whet[h]er the vessel was still afloat.

Wood and water have been delayed on frivolous pretenses.

In Europe and from powerful nations all this would be cause of war.

By evasions and double dealing the Government of Loo-Choo invites rudeness or the exercise of force.

They cannot apparently be moved by their own reason to comply with their aggreements but think an excuse answers every purpose.—Truth is a great virtue, and the people of America hate and despise duplicity.

The Loo-Chooans do not seem capable of carrying out their treaty stipulations. I shall recommend to my Government to place a Consul here, so as to obviate their remissness.

It does not make any difference as to who is the particular person in the wrong.

I have tried to avoid any rudeness to the Loo-Choo Government, and my unwillingness has been taken for want of power; my passing over foolish excuses, for blindness in perceiving their folly.

If they would avoid very serious difficulty, they must supply vessels promptly and not seek to annoy with foolish speeches.

DOCUMENT MARKED B.

U.S. Ship Vincennes
To the Honourable Secretary of State   Kago Sima Bay
    for Foreign Affairs   January 4, 1855
    Kingdom of Japan

Sir!

The Government of the United States sent five vessels, of which this is the chief, to examine the dangers of the Ocean. We have been round more than half the Globe. We have at last arrived at one of the Japanese ports. If the Islands of Japan with the rocks and shoals which surround them, were out of the paths which our vessels follow across the Ocean, the world could say nothing, but as these dangers remain in the road of ships, we must examine them, and tell our countrymen where they lie. Otherwise our vessels would be wrecked, and many valuable lives might be lost.

We find our way across seas by certain instruments and observations of heavenly bodies. But as some of the instruments, called chronometers, are liable to go wrong, it is absolutely necessary to make examinations from time to time, of whether they perform well, and to correct their rates.

It happens, that the astronomical observations for the error of these instruments must be made on the land, because a vessel is too unsteady for very delicate observations.

Why need friends hesitate to speak plainly? From want of clearness and of mutual understanding, difficulties arise. We must go on shore to take astronomical observations.

We are in distress without them!

I am sure that the Government of Japan, and my own Government, would not thank any Japanese officer who should compel me to use force in taking necessary astronomical observations.

I say this because in a few months my own vessel, or one or more of those under my command, will, in the prosecution of our duties, probably stop at some port in Japan, and I earnestly hope no too ardent officer will by his overzeal bring himself and me into trouble.

I have the honour to be

your respectful friend,

(signed) JOHN RODGERS, U.S.N.
Commanding U.S. Surveying Expedition
to the North Pacific Ocean &c

DOCUMENT MARKED C.[29]

Honourable Secretary of State
of the Empire of Japan

U.S. Ship Vincennes
Hong Kong
February 7, 1855

Sir!

The Government of Japan is probably aware that five vessels were sent from the United States two years ago to make surveys of the unknown rocks, shoals, and islands in the way of their commerce.

We have at last arrived at Japan. A very extensive trade is now carried on between our possessions on the Pacific and China. A glance at the map shows that since your Kingdom lies between those countries, our ships must necessarily pass by it.

No commerce can be secure until the dangers in the route it takes are explored and placed on charts. Our ships in pursuing their lawful commerce run many risks from unsurveyed

[29] This second letter addressed to the "Honourable Secretary of State of the Empire of Japan" was not drafted until Rodgers' return to Hongkong. It was delivered to the governors of the treaty-port of Shimoda in May of the same year. The earlier letter had been delivered to unknown authorities off the town of Yamagawa in Kagōshima Bay.

dangers, which surround your islands. Can a friendly power wish to keep those dangers hidden?

If our vessels should continue to remain in ignorance of the perils to be shun[n]ed, many of them would be wrecked, many innocent lives would be lost, many unwilling guests would be thrown upon Japanese hospitality; expenses would be incurred, and vexations encountered.

These causes seem to render a survey as desirable to the Japanese as to ourselves. There are other reasons for anticipating their cordial co-operation with us.

By the 10th article of the treaty with the United States of America our vessels in case of absolute distress have a right to enter Japanese ports.

It is a rule in the interpretation of treaties amongst nations, and a rule too of natural reason, that any right conferred involves the session of such powers as are necessary and proper to the enjoyment of the right—that a permission given supposes also consent to do those things without which the permission could not be used. To tell a friend that he might enter the nearest harbor in case his vessel were sinking or on fire or dismasted or the crew starving, but to hide from him the position of the harbor, and the way to enter it, would seem more like mockery than good faith.

It thus appears by a fair, obvious and usual interpretation that the Japanese have already given to us the permission we now ask. Nor could it be supposed even had this clause not existed in their treaty that they would wish to keep their rocks and shoals as hidden pitfalls to the commerce, and to the lives of the citizens of a great power with which they had entered into friendly relations, and mutual good offices. This they would do by preventing us from learning the position of these dangers, and thereby knowing how to avoid them. The knowledge we seek cannot injure the Japanese. It is of the highest moment to us. The governments of Europe and of the United States carefully prepare charts of all their harbors, these charts are published, and agents in foreign countries sell them. It is not found by experience that this course has any bad effects, and it offers many advantages. The governments do more than this; they anchor light-vessels on shoals, and put light-houses to work on dangerous rocks, to warn off incautious mariners, or guide the distressed ones safely. Humanity and policy here go hand in hand.

War-vessels can find their way without charts. By keeping armed boats a short distance ahead, under the protection of their guns they can explore passages however tortuous; by signals they can converse, and night offers no hindrance to their operations. War-vessels in an enemy's harbor often prefer the mask of night for making surveys, to open day. With peaceful merchant-vessels the case is widely different. They need charts to guide and instruct them.

I humbly beg the Mighty Japanese Government to permit me to survey in Japanese waters. We have no hidden purposes, no views which we do not avow. I shall be most happy to receive on board any two officers whom they may designate to accompany us. They will see our operations, learn our methods, and can have copies of our work.

You will perceive that the arguments I use are necessity, our treaty, your friendship, and the natural right which every nation has, in common with every private individual, to examine hidden dangers lying in the road which may lawfully be followed. It has been the custom to make surveys of distant seas and islands before they were frequented, and before the necessity arose for a knowledge of them, in order that vessels driven out of their course might still have the means of safety. In the present case the necessity came before the survey is asked for. It is only after the Japanese islands have become an obstruction and danger to our vessels in their daily route, that we ask to examine them. In this your government will see a moderation going out of its customary path, and using delay, while in other cases surveys had hastened before trade.

The arguments are so strong that I dare not anticipate the consequences of refusal. Certainly the President of the United

States can not regard such refusal as a proof of good will on the part of the government of Japan.

It may be prudent to say in conclusion that I have come to Simoda to confer with the supreme authorities. Of course I can not refer our treaty, nor our rights under the treaty to the petty local magistrates. Our conduct shall in every case be orderly, decorus and respectful. But any obstructions or unasked interference on their part will induce me to treat them as violators of the 4th article of the treaty,[30] as alike enemies of the Emperor of Japan and the President of the United States.

I have the honour to be
very respectfully
your sincere friend,
(signed) JOHN RODGERS
Commanding U.S. Surveying
Expedition to the North Pacific
To the Honourable Secretary   Ocean.
of State
of the Empire of Japan.

In a letter to Secretary Dobbin, dated Hongkong, February 15, 1855, Commander Rodgers deplores the lack of information concerning the *Porpoise*, which had not been seen since the previous September twenty-first, when she parted company from the *Vincennes* near the Pescadores Islands, between Formosa and the Chinese mainland. Rodgers had inquired of crews who had visited Guam and certain of the Caroline Islands, but without success.

As the expedition was being prepared for its major operations around the main Japanese islands, its commander shipped home several kinds of scientific collections already obtained. Among these were: a list of numerous varieties of packaged seeds on their way to the National Botanical Garden in Washington; a report on the flora of

[30] Article IV of Perry's Treaty of Kanagawa (March 31, 1854) reads: "Those Shipwrecked persons and other Citizens of the United States shall be free as in other Countries, and not subjected to confinement, but shall be amenable to just laws." See Hunter Miller (ed.), *Treaties and Other International Acts of the United States of America*, VI, p. 441. Washington, Government Printing Office, 1942. Rodgers was exceeding any normal interpretation of this article, which had been designed to cover the treatment of shipwrecked or stranded American whalers and other seamen.

Peel Island (the major island of the Bonin group) and of the Liu Ch'ius; together with a rather short list of zoological specimens (forwarded from Hongkong on March 14, 1855); some three thousand such specimens belonging to 1,153 distinct species had previously been sent and had been covered by a report dated Hongkong, January 29, 1855.

In a hermetically sealed tin box Rodgers forwarded from Hongkong to Secretary Dobbin (April 2, 1855) most of the charts resulting from the last voyages, that is, since the previous September. The list follows:

1. South Extreme of Japan and the islands toward Loo-Choo
2. Asses Ears and Vincennes Rocks
3. Ousima & Kakirouma
4. Bay of Kago Sima and on Kiushu
5. Bay of Sima-u in Ou-sima
6. Lloyd's Harbor in the Bonin Islands, (unfinished)
7. Sketch of Lot's Wife [an island]
8. Reconnaissance of Borodino Islands
9. ditto of Rosario Island
10. A reduction of No. 1, 2, & 3 on one sheet (for immediate publication)
11. Bullocks Harbor
12. Bar and Mouth of the Teen-Tsin Ho [Peiho] (the two latter made by the steamer John Hancock and Schooner Fenimore Cooper).

Commander Rodgers informed his superior in Washington (Hongkong, April 2, 1855) that he had been obliged to charter a vessel to take supplies northward to Hakodaté. The captain of the brig *Greta*, of Hamburg, had agreed to make the trip for five thousand dollars; he had been instructed to fly the American flag in Japanese waters.

U.S. Ship Vincennes
Hong Kong
[Secretary Dobbin]   April 2d, 1855
Sir!

The Steamer Hancock and Schooner Fenimore Cooper have sailed. I enclose copies of their instructions. [A paragraph here omitted explains that there are a number of affairs which must be completed before the flagship can sail.]

We shall pursue the objects which I formerly sketched, a recapitulation may be proper.

The Vincennes will meet the Cooper and Hancock at Loo-Choo. They will probably have finished some work in the vicinity by the time of my arrival. Together we will thence survey the chain of Islands towards Japan. From the southern extreme of Japan, we shall push on to Simoda, in order to confer with the Japanese government, so that such obstructions as we met at Yama Gawa, in Kago-Sima Bay, may not be repeated. On the 15th of May we meet in Hakodadi, [the] Cooper will survey the Kurile, or Fox Islands [sic], to Petropaulaski. The Cooper there seperates from us, after we have filled her up with provisions from the Vincennes. She takes up the survey of the Aleutian Islands, and she also searches for the crew of the ship Monongahela. We go into the Arctic Sea.

We shall meet at San Francisco in October next, where I hope to have the honor of hearing from you.

It is to be regretted that the John Hancock is not a better vessel. She had to be strengthened in Shanghai, by iron knees. Her bulk heads fell down for want of proper strength in her construction. Her model is very defective. She is eminently unfit for her work. She is however, in jealous hands, and she will achieve what she can.

It is sad to say all this but it is proper to say it.

I hope you will give me authority to sell her after our arrival in China, from San Francisco.[31]

I have the honor to be

Very Respectfully
Your Obdt Servt,

JOHN RODGERS

To Honorable James C. Dobbin
Secretary of the Navy
Washington, D.C.

Comdg. U.S. Surveying Expedition to North Pacific Ocean.
&c &c

[31] Commander Rodgers had already announced his intention to complete the cruise northward and in the following year (1856) to survey three routes from San Francisco across the Pacific in the direction of Shanghai. This plan was not modified until, apparently, revised instructions from Washington reached him upon his arrival at San Francisco.

It is unnecessary to quote from Commander Rodgers' instructions to Acting Lieutenant William Gibson in command of the schooner *Fenimore Cooper*. These orders parallel the explanation given to Secretary Dobbin in the previous letter.

In his directions to Lieutenant H. K. Stevens of the *John Hancock*, Rodgers ordered him to accompany the *Fenimore Cooper* proceeding between Formosa and the coast of China, stopping at several of the Pescadores Islands for the making of surveys. Thence he should sail to Naha in the Liu Ch'ius, and from there he should strike westward for basic surveying of the Amakirima group. Later on the reunited squadron would survey more closely the "chain of islands between Loo-Choo and Japan." There follows an excerpt from these instructions.

... From Tanega Sima on the most northern of these islands we shall push on to "Simoda" and make terms with the Government, for the continuance of our work. We should lose time and prestige in dealing with the village authorities, who are not responsible to our government for their conduct. On May 15th you will endeavour to be in Hakodadi where you will find provisions and coal in a transport chartered for the purpose of supplying us.

The degree of freedom with which we shall survey in Japanese waters will depend in a great measure upon the terms which I shall obtain at Simoda. While I shall maintain without any reservation the right to survey, I shall be very careful in exercising this right and by all becoming means endeavour to soothe the jealousy of the Japanese. You will readily understand that this is an occasion in which caution, forebearance and delicacy must be exercised even in carrying out a right. Any collision would be deeply deplorable. From "Simoda" I shall be better able to point out the field of your labor, than from this place. I shall be inclined however to send you around the island of Kiusiu [Kyūshū] through the straits of Corea and thus to Hakodadi. From Hakodadi around the western coast of Yeso or Matsmai along the eastern side of Saghalien to the river Amour. The Amour is one of the great rivers of the world. It is the largest stream which empties into the vast Pacific. It is the great highway of natures making from the shores of the Pacific to the centre of Asia and at some future day a vast commerce will doubtless be borne upon its waters. A town at its mouth seems the Russian Sister of San Francisco. . . .

It is not certainly known whether Saghalien is an island or a peninsula.[32] There are authorities on both sides and the charts give both views. I believe that there is a passage for ships through the Gulf of Tartary into the Sea of Okhotsk. From the Amour you can easily resolve this important doubt. It will be desirable to join a survey through this passage to the end of La Perouses labors in the Gulf of Tartary in about the latitude of 51° 40'. If there be a passage for ships it is most valuable. As it is quite certain that the waters of the Amour ran out to the Northward, the current must be a great obstruction to sailing vessels approaching the mouth of the river against it. . . .

Stevens was further directed to proceed from the mouth of the Amur River to survey the shores of the Sea of Okhotsk, whence the *John Hancock* was to reach San Francisco, if possible, by October 15, 1855. Commander Rodgers remarked that existing information was very vague about such characteristics of the Sea of Okhotsk as longitudes, harbors, direction and strength of currents, prevalence of fogs, direction and character of winds, and range of thermometer.

Acting Lieutenant Gibson described for Rodgers (Naha, April 26, 1855) the *Fenimore Cooper's* voyage after she left Hongkong on March 23rd. The coast of Formosa had been skirted on the way to Great Liu Ch'iu; the report is crowded with marine information concerning weather and hydrography.

[32] The Japanese and Russians probably were aware of the insular nature of Sakhalin by the very early years of the nineteenth century. Russian explorations were becoming more frequent, and these led to quickened Japanese relations with Sakhalin and the Kurile Islands. These were the years of Inō Chukei's geographical activities.

[Secretary Dobbin]   June 11th, 1855
Sir:

We found upon our arrival in Simoda, ten Americans residing in the Temple of Yokushen, five Gentlemen, three ladies, and two children.

The enterprize of my countrymen in thus colonizing Japan, so soon after the treaty, has forced upon my attention some subjects which I beg leave to discuss. I am aware that my remarks may seem to want becomeing diffidence. But my convictions are strong, and though my conclusions may be rejected, my end will be attained should I draw attention to the points which struck me while on the spot.

More than 40 whalers will probably winter in Hakodadi. Whaling crews have the reputation of too often behaving riotously on shore. Some American authority should be there to redress wrongs which they may receive, or do. Without this, our treaty of peace may lead us very wide of the end it professes.

There is no provision in the treaty for a Consul at Hakodadi.[33] A man of war with a judicious Commander should be sent there to winter. It would be well to keep such a vessel in that port, until circumstances do away with the necessity for one.

The Consul at Simoda will be the highest Officer accredited to the Japanese government. His duties will often lead him to treat directly with the authorities at Jeddo. From the circumstances of the case, it appears necessary he should have jurisdiction over the delinquencies of our countrymen, and the right to appeal to Jeddo for redress of their wrongs. Neither prisoner[s], nor witnesses, can be conveniently sent home for trial.[34]

[33] On May 1, 1857, Elisha E. Rice opened the office of a commercial agent at Hakodaté. The choice of this man was unfortunate, as Consul-General Townsend Harris was to learn.

[34] In this letter Rodgers specifically suggested the establishment of extrater-

Commodore Perry answered in reply to the question, "What is the rank of a Consul?" that the Consul ranked about with the Governor of Simoda. The Governor of Simoda is a Prince, and was one of the Imperial Commissioners. The highest Officer accredited to an Empire, and treating directly with the supreme government, has the duties of an Embassador, or minister. Even if the Consul be only [a] Judge it would be scarcely decorus that he should meddle personally with trade. His cases will principally be commercial ones, and his duties will often call him to decide upon interests which may be his own. Merchants in Japan are placed low in the social scale, below a private in the army. No single American however worthy can reasonably hope to overcome the prejudices of caste in a nation so wedded to its forms, its habits of thought, and its customs.

It is not expedient that the Consul should gain his living by means which those whom he wishes to influence consider disreputable. The Consul General to some of the Barbary States holds apparently an official position and receives a salary, closely corresponding to what seems suitable for our Consul at Simoda. Our consuls in China have the necessary Judicial powers. The treaty provides for Consuls, at Simoda. It may have reference I presume to a Vice Consul, to perform the usual duties of Consul, and to receive the fees of office.[35]

ritoriality covering American citizens in Japan as in China. Actually this should already have accrued to the United States by the most-favored-nation clause of the Treaty of Kanagawa, since the Russian Admiral Count E. V. Putiatin had, on February 7, 1855, concluded a treaty at Shimoda. Article VIII of this agreement provided for the substance of extraterritoriality. See the treaty text in J. H. Gubbins, *The Progress of Japan, 1853-1871*, Appendix 5, p. 237. Oxford, Clarendon Press, 1911.

Extraterritoriality in Japan for American citizens was embodied in the Convention for Further Regulating the Intercourse of American Citizens within the Empire of Japan, concluded at the instance of Townsend Harris at Shimoda on June 17, 1857. See, Hunter Miller (ed.), *Treaties and Other International Acts. . .* , VII, p. 595. In still greater detail was it stipulated in Articles Sixth and Seventh of the Treaty of Yedo (July 29, 1858). See, *ibid.*, pp. 955-957.

[35] The reference here is to Article XI of the Treaty of Kanagawa. See, Hunter Miller (ed.), *Treaties and Other International Acts. . .* , VI, p. 442. A consul or agent was not to be stationed at Shimoda until eighteen months had

The Consul and Vice Consul might be associated, if deemed expedient, to try Americans. Were the Governor of the Port added, they might form a mixed court for cases occurring between Japanese and Americans.

The currency needs regulating. One dollar of our money passes in all purchases for an Itzebue, which weighs rather less than the third of a dollar. The government takes the dollars, and pays an equal number of itzebues to the tradesmen. It thus realizes a profit of more than two hundred per cent upon all American purchases. The rule does well at present, for the profit induces the government to encourage buying.

It has built a Bazaar for the exclusive use of foreigners, and the shops in it are filled with rich goods.

I was told by some of the Russian Officers who had seen the magnificent presents to their Emperor, that many of the articles in the Bazaar were of the best quality. The Merchants there are very anxious to sell: they crowd around us and solicit our custom. "You come to my shop" is repeated on every side. Most of them speak enough English to be understood. The novelty, the scarcity, and the innate beauty of Japanese ware, may now pay the American Merchant for his outlay—but no permanent trade can continue on such a basis.

The Government refused to take gold in payment for the Hancocks coal. By my direction Capt. Stevens left it to them to refuse gold if they chose. That the subject would be referred to the government of the United States. He accordingly offered them gold, and told them that if they refused it, he would pay silver. The Governor after mature deliberation, concluded to take which ever Capt. Stevens decided to give, and the bill was by mutual agreement paid, half in silver, half in gold. The treaty says we "shall be permitted to exchange gold, and silver coin," under such regulations as shall

elapsed after the treaty's signature. Townsend Harris, a merchant of New York, was appointed the first United States Consul-General to Japan. He arrived at Shimoda aboard the U.S.S. *San Jacinto* on August 21, 1856.

be temporarily established by the Japanese government for that purpose. This leaves with the Japanese apparently, the right to put their own value, upon our gold. The relative value of gold and silver in Japan has always been different from that established in Europe. In Japan twelve of silver, is about worth one of gold. In Europe seventeen for one will not differ much from the truth. As silver is dearer in Japan than with us, and gold cheaper, Silver will be the more profitible basis for mutual adjustment of the currency. There is great avidity for foreign articles, and the government is I am sure, the only bar to extensive foreign trade. The treaty says, we "shall be permitted to exchange articles or goods for other articles of goods." This at present is utterly forbidden.[36] No Japanese Merchant can get permission to exchange goods, and no one dare do it without permission. It might be sound policy to request the Japanese to impose duties—say ten per cent on imports—ten per cent on exports, and a tonnage duty of ten cents per ton.[37]

No trade in Japan can flourish except by the acquiescence of the government. In offering inducements to the government, for it to foster buying, and selling, by giving it a direct profit on sales, and purchases—we would best forward our own views. Nothing can be done except with the government. The government will do nothing in good faith except it be interested. Their treaty with us was I think dictated by apprehension of some greater evil. The buoys in Simoda are not in place. There is reason for thinking they were taken up. Pilots came on board after the vessel had anchored.

[36] The currency question is discussed in the editor's forthcoming book entitled "The Dynamics of American Expansion toward Japan, 1791-1860," Chapters XIII to XVI.

Rodgers was quoting from Article VII of the Treaty of Kanagawa. See Hunter Miller (ed.), *Treaties and Other International Acts*, VI, p. 440.

[37] By the Treaty of Yedo, July 29, 1858, Townsend Harris obtained a tariff schedule, which was later modified by implementation of the most-favored-nation principle. See, Articles Fourth and Eleventh of the treaty and Additional Regulations Third and Seventh in *ibid.*, VII, pp. 953-954, 959, 967-969, 971-973.

Our Whalers have already made arrangements to resort in large numbers to Hakodadi. This will require a large increase of police force on the part of the Japanese. Whalers do not trade, and it would be bad policy to make so great a convenience to us an unmitigated tax to the Japanese.

Ten cents per ton will be a moderate charge, and may perhaps cover the expense to the Japanese. I am afraid they might not understand that they receive more than comes directly into their hands. In thus leading a nation so young in all that relates to foreign intercourse we may forestal injurious action after they become more versed in foreign usages.

The Harbor of Heda, about thirty miles farther from the sea than Simoda, is secure, and well sheltered. The Harbor of Simoda is very unsafe in the SW Monsoon. With bad holding ground, it is entirely open to the Southward. It has two sunken rocks in it. The Russians endeavoured without success to substitute Heda for Simoda in their treaty.

If the treaty be revised with a large force to give weight to the discussion—we may I think carry that, or any other reasonable point. Words without the authority of many cannon will avail little. I think this statement is a clue upon which every thing turns. It might be well to obtain the assent of England, and Russia, to the change of Simoda for Heda. I understand the Japanese told the Russians that they could not take Simoda from us, and that opening Heda to them would add to their expenses those of another imperial city.

The government of Japan taken somewhat by surprize, does not seem to be sensible of the advantages to be reaped by the residence in their midst of our countrymen and women. It has ordered them away. I think it will not force them to go.

I enclose the correspondence between the Governor of Simoda, and the American gentlemen resident there, and a copy of my letter to the Governor in relation thereto. I need not say how earnestly I hope that my views may be approved.

The Russians found that Osacka, said to be the principal

commercial town of the Empire, can be approached within three miles by ships. Lighterage would be easy. I consider the Bay of Kago Sima, from its position, of extreme importance to our trade with Shanghai. Ships would lose no distance in calling there.

I would call the attention of any future commissioner to Japan to the 32d article of the American treaty with China. It is stated in Lieut. Forbe's "Five Years in China," Page 2-34, that the English supplementary treaty has a clause admitting surveying foreign ships into the inner waters of the coast, provided the Emperor has a faithful copy of the result. As Lieut. Forbes and his brother officers surveyed under such an agreement, he is doubtless right in the main fact of such permission having been given, though I have not been able to find any such clause in the published supplement treaty between Great Britain and China.[38]

You will perceive by the unwillingness of the Japanese to trade for goods, by pilots not coming on board vessels, by their sending spies to accompany the Russians, by their forbidding to the Common people all intercourse with us, by there [sic] ordering the Americans in Simoda to leave, by their not replacing buoys, that they gave way to Commodore Perry rather from the force of circumstances than from any change in their wishes for national isolation.

What they gave was unwillingly bestowed, and as much as they can, will be gradually withdrawn.

[38] For Article XXXII of the Sino-American Treaty of Wanghsia, July 3, 1844, see, Hunter Miller (ed.), *Treaties and Other International Acts. . . ,* IV, p. 569.

The only Anglo-Chinese agreement touching on the matter to which Rodgers here referred is to be found in Annex 2, General Regulations, XIV, July 1843. This merely provided that the British government might station a cruiser at each of the five opened treaty-ports, and that such warships would not have to pay port fees or dues. This was confirmed by the Treaty of the Bogue, October 8, 1843, and was reiterated in Article X of this document. See, Lewis Hertslet (ed.), . . . *Treaties and Conventions . . . between Great Britain and Foreign Powers. . . ,* VI, pp. 248, 265. London, Henry Butterworth and James Bigg and Son, 1845.

With our eyes open, it will be our own fault, if we stumble in our negotiations.

I have the honor to be

Very Respectfully
Your Obdt Servt,

JOHN RODGERS
Comdg. U.S. Surveying Expedition,
to the North Pacific Ocean &c.

Honorable James C. Dobbin
Secretary of the Navy
Washington, D.C.

While the squadron was anchored in Shimoda's harbor, Rodgers' intention to despatch the *John Hancock* to survey the port of Heda provoked the following exchange of informal memoranda. As explained in the editor's introduction, a group of Russians had been stranded when their frigate, the *Diana*, had foundered after a tidal wave. They were subsequently quartered at Heda, which is on the Bay of Sūrūga.

[An unsigned memorandum submitted to Commander Rodgers at Shimoda by the Japanese interpreter Hori Tatsunosuke]

The proposition to go to Hedi and visit the Russians has been made at the convention the day before yesterday but since it was communicated that this proposition cannot be permitted, so it speaks for itself, that the passage cannot take place.

Afterwards it was again asked, and explained, that the visit to the Russians was founded upon friendship, that the arrival of American vessels must have been expected from the notification of Commdre. Perry of last year, and that the necessity of a survey of all coasts had been stated in the letter lately handed over, and read, so there could be no objection to the trip to Hedi.

But of American ships has been nothing heard, and besides it the acquiescence of the government to the just mentioned written petition is very uncertain. So the trip to Hedi, and the survey of its harbor, cannot take place.

Should it have become necessary to communicate with the Russians, they shall be called here to this place.

This word is communicated in writing that no misunderstanding might take place.

The 4th Sigreato [Fourth Month].

By intention, Rodgers' reply to the document quoted above was given no date or signature. It was enclosed in an envelope labelled simply "Memorandum."

The Memorandum has been received, and its contents have been noted. A letter was sent to Jeddo to ask permission to survey in Japanese waters.[39] It is not thought that the Government of Japan would wish to give our vessels permission to enter their harbors in case of distress, and then refuse to let them know where the harbors may be found. According to the manner of thinking in Europe, and the United States, this would not be just nor fair.

If the Japanese were to offer a man food, and then not let him know where to get it, would it be thought fair, and that the offer of food was in good faith?

A vessel cannot go into a port unless she knows where to find it, any more than a man can eat, without food.

This however is to be decided, and a letter was written to

[39] Rodgers here referred to his communication to the "Honourable Secretary of State of the Empire of Japan," written in February but submitted at Shimoda in May, 1855.

find what the Japanese Government intends. No one knows better than the Japanese the obligations of friendship; Americans have read of heroic friendship in Japan. The following sentence is from a book published in America, "It is represented there is no peril a Japanese will not encounter to serve a friend. No torture will compel him to betray a trust, and even the stranger who seeks his aid, will be protected to the last drop of his blood." We have read of Tchouya and his wife and admired them as setting an example worthy of all imitation, and admiration.

Now the Russians are in distress. The Russian Emperor is the friend of our President, and our President is his friend. The two countries are at peace, and in friendship. Were the Japanese wrecked in Russia, and far from their country, If the Americans were coming to Japan they would go to see the Japanese that they might tell their countrymen they were well, that they had been seen, and that they were in a comfortable situation.

Now it is not expedient to talk about the Treaty. That must be discussed in Jeddo, but the treaty does not talk about the duties of friendship, and we can discuss that.

The American Commodore has power to ask permission to survey where he wishes, but has the Governor of Simoda power to refuse him permission, or to grant it to him for other parts of the Empire of Japan? Therefore the American Commodore would rather talk about his friendship for the Russians. Both countries permit friendship, and admire heroic examples of it.

Besides how can anyone refuse permission under the treaty without knowing that his government wishes him to do so. It is a very small matter. The port is known. It has been surveyed. Vessels have been into it.

To so great a government a small steamer going into a known port is of little moment, and whether the Hancock goes or does not go, is not worthy of any long discussion.

If after the Hancock is in Heda, and she has seen the Russians, should it be agreed to carry them away, then it will be done.

The *John Hancock's* visit to Heda, in the principality of Idzū, is described in Lieutenant Stevens' report of June 9, 1855, which is quoted extensively below.

The next document reveals the Japanese objections against another plan proposed by Commander Rodgers: to send a launch close along the coast of eastern Japan between Shimoda and Hakodaté for purposes of charting and general observations.

His Excellency Commander John Rodgers

My Sir!

It has been said that some of your squadron on their voyage North want to sail in a boat along the coast of our Empire, and that if wanting water it run into the nearest harbor. On the ground of the treaty with the U.S. our nation is of opinion that the ships of the U.S. are allowed no other harbors than those of Simoda, and Hakodadi, except in storm or in distress. Should a vessel wantonly run into any harbor it cannot be sure that there may not occur unpleasant difficulties, and our friendship might be really weakened. So it is impossible to concur in your wish to run into other harbors as long as there is not given a favorable, or unfavorable answer, to your written application, which shortly ago was handed to the Government.

The 10th of the 4th Month 1855

> (Signed) Izawa Mimasakanokami
> [Izawa Mimasaka-no-kami]
>
> (Signed) Tsoedzoeki Soerroeganokami
> [Suzuki Sūrūga-no-kami]
>
> (Signed) Inowoeje Sinjemon
> [Inouye Sinyemon]

The busy cruise of Lieutenant Stevens commanding the *John Hancock* between Hongkong, which he left on March 22, 1855, and Hakodaté was covered in his report to Commander Rodgers (Hakodaté, June 9, 1855). During parts of the voyage the steamer was separated from the *Fenimore Cooper* and from the *Vincennes*. Her skipper mentioned meeting on one of the Pescadores a mandarin, presumably a Chinese official. Parts of his description of Formosa together with the latter portion of his letter are worth quoting:

On the 28th we sailed [from the Pescadores] intending to touch along the NW part of Formosa, but a fresh gale prevented our communicating with the shore, and finally induced me to proceed to the Srd, where under the lee of the land we found smooth weather.

On the 30th we passed close by the Island of Lambay, which together with the adjoining coast of Formosa, was incorrectly laid down on our charts; a survey was therefore commenced and carried on under the direction of Mr. Carnes, assisted by the other officers, I being too unwell to attend to it myself.

That evening we anchored off the town of Pong Lieu, in a very good roadstead, affording good shelter in the NE Monsoon. Enquiry was also made here, but with equally fruitless result regarding the Porpoise. Painful as the conclusion is, it seems but too certain, that she is lost for ever, and that the Noble Spirits on board of her, will be heard of no more.

On the 31st we proceeded down the coast about 20 miles, but the weather came on so bad that we were induced to anchor in a small bay, where we found good shelter about a mile from shore, in 6 faths. of water, being protected from all winds with Easting in them.

This bay has two Chinese villages on it, which are the most southern of their settlements, and there they seem [to] wage a continual warfare with the Natives, whom they describe as Canibals. Their village was surrounded by a wall and the people all went armed, ready for immediate resistance, while a strong watch was always kept over their cattle to prevent their being driven off by the Natives.

Mr. Hartman, the Draughtsman, saw some of the natives, whom he describes as perfect savages. He succeded in obtaining a bow and some arrows from them, which are on board this vessel at the disposition of the Government.

On the 2nd the weather changed and allowed us to proceed; we continued our examination around the Cape and up along the East coast as high as Latitude 22° 22′ N. When bad weather again set in, and forced us off the coast. . . .

The western coast of Formosa, as far as we saw of it, is of moderate height with gentle slopes to the water and abounding in fine vallies, while the East coast rises suddenly from the sea in many places to mountains of great height, and affords comparatively few places fit for cultivation. There are, however, two large vallies, one just North of Souau Bay, and the other not far to the Srd of it, at River Pt. All the other vallies that we saw were small and shut in by high ranges of hills. The whole island though seems well wooded and is every where covered with verdure. . . .

Rather complex, data-laden descriptions of islands scattered from Formosa to Great Liu Ch'iu (Okinawa) and of others farther in a northeastward direction need not detain us. We pick up the story of the *John Hancock* and her crew at Tanegashima—just southeast of the major Japanese island of Kyūshū.

The next day, May 9th, we examined the West-side of Tanega-Sima. There is a small bay just opposite Seriphos, which would afford anchorage for a few vessels. We did not go into it however, but only looked in at the entrance and hauled out again.

The next day we sighted the South Cape of Sikokf [Shikoku] Island (Asisurinomo-sake or Cape Tōsa) and found it some miles to the Srd of its position on the chart. It is a high bold cape. We sighted other points along the coast, but not near enough to fix them.

May 13th while standing for the land, we made the Vincennes ahead. That evening we followed you in and anchored in Simoda Bay. During the passage up from Tanega-Sima we had a strong NE current until we reached Lat 33°, but after that felt very little current in any direction. Along the land the wind was variable and often light with much thick weather.

May 21st we sailed for the harbour of Hade [Heda] in the bay of Foutcheou [Sūrūga] and examined the coast between Simoda and that place. The Master's report of Lat & Long will give its position.

We remained in Hade May 24th, the weather being too bad to do any thing. From the Russians there I obtained a tracing of their survey of the Harbour. It was not complete, having no topography, but as the soundings had been taken with great care, I adopted it, and proved the shore line, and fixed some few hills by a base from altitude of mast and length of ship.

The harbour is about a mile across at its greatest length, and the water deep, having from 19 to 24 faths. in the middle of the Bay.

The entrance is narrow, but as the distance is so short, it is easy of access, and its narrowness makes the harbour quite secure, even from NW Winds, to which direction it is open. The South point of the entrance is low, but covered with trees, and its outer part piled up with shingle. The North point rises in a steep bluff, with red cliffs on the outer part, forming a good mark for the harbour. There are also some red cliffs just to the Srd and the entrance is between the two; from the red cliffs to the Srd the land trends to the S.Erd, forming a bight. But there is no place in the neighbourhood, that could be mistaken for Hade. As there are high bluffs on both sides of it, the coast trending nearly NNE and being quite straight until the entrance is opened. About 2 and ½ miles to the Nrd, the coast bends sharp to the Erd, forming a rounded point with some green bushes on the end of it, the high land sloping gradually to the water and the point rounding off showes much the same from different points to the SWrd. This also forms a good mark for the harbour. High hills extend both North and South of the bay, coming down with steep bluffs to the water, but to the Eastward there is a pretty valley with several streams running from it.

The town is at the mouth of this valley and containes about 300 houses. The people seem poor, but they have there an abundance of poultry, which we have not met with elsewhere.

In the interior there is a conical mountain, which brought to bear ESE, leads into the harbour. Fuse [Fuji-yama] N ¼ W leads also into it.

Leaving Hada [Heda] on the 15th, we crossed the Bay of Foutcheou (or Futsiu) and looked into a fine large bay, about West from Hada. The body of the bay is open to the NE, but a projecting point affords shelter; several junks were anchored behind it, but there appeared to be no town just there, though there were several all around the other parts of the bay. As for us, [we found] . . . 8 faths. good holding ground. Returned to Simoda that night.

April 27th on offering gold in payment of the ship's bills, it was refused by the Japanese, and they went on shore. On the morning of the 28th they came off again, and after some talk they said the Governor had ordered them not to take gold.

The Vincennes had got under way, but was still in sight. I therefore made signal to her and pulled out to communicate with you [Rodgers]. On our return the Japanese had gone on shore again, though they had been offered the silver if they positively refused the gold. They afterwards agreed to take which ever I chose to give them, and by mutual agreement took half gold and half silver.

Though at the time they were told, that if they still refused the gold, they might have all silver. By their account gold was only worth 855 cash to the dollar, and they expressed a wish, that there should be some mutual agreement as to the value at which it should be received.

Sailed from Simoda on the 29th and cut in the Islands off Jeddo Bay, except Oho-sima which was not visible. On the

30th passed round Fatsisjo, and fixed it, but could see no other land, as it was hazy. This island differs from the representation on any chart, and there are some triffling differences in the other islands.

From Fatsisjo, we came direct to Hakodadi, passing the Vincennes on the morning of the 3rd of June, and anchoring here the night of the 4th. The weather was very thick all the last part of the run, so that we could do nothing. This work has all been plotted. You will see that this vessel has been actively employed, and I would do injustice to both officers and men were I to neglect to mention the readiness I have met in them to carry forward the work.

I forward to you the Master's report of Lat and Long and Abstract of the Log.

I have the honor to be

Respectfully etc.

H. K. STEVENS
Lieut. Commanding

To
Lt. John Rodgers
Commandg. Expedition
to the North Pacific Ocean, &c.

An engineer from the steamer *John Hancock* appended, in the form of a brief report to his superior, his analysis of two samples of bituminous coal, one from Formosa, the other from Kyūshū.

[Commander John Rodgers]

U.S. Schr. Fenimore Cooper
Hakodadi
June 9th, 1855.

Sir:

We arrived in this port on the 6th of this month, our cruise since leaving Loo-Choo having been in the main successful. I cannot say entirely so; for, in some of the most interesting localities, the weather was as unfavorable as possible. Leaving Napa-kiang in company, on the morning of the 27th April, the schooner passed, agreeably to instructions between Igousho, or Sugar Loaf, and the main islands. The channel is narrow. Off the north point of Sugar Loaf island a reef extends eastward about half a mile; and along the Loo-Chooan side of the passage are several reefs and sand banks. At 8 P.M. we hove to near the north cape of Loo-Choo.

On the 28th we reconnoitered the eastern sides of Yourou and Oukin, and the southern side of Kakirouma. Off Yourou a reef stretches one mile and a half from the NE point, and there is one of less extent from the SE point. Oukin is bolder of approach, and Kakirouma has blue water up to the rocks. All these islands are more or less cultivated, and are partially wooded. We saw scattered houses on the first two, and a village on the latter, prettily situated in a cluster of trees on a hill top. Saw a junk at Oukin and one at Kakirouma hauled up by hawsers upon the beach. Off the South Cape of Kakirouma we communicated with the Vincennes.[40]

On the 29th followed the eastern side of Kakirouma within a half and a quarter of a mile distance, observing two deep bays, with cultivated slopes and villages, and several junks moored. Then we crossed over to Ou-sima, passing closely eastward of Middle rocks. At 4 P.M. entered the passage between the main land of Ou-sima and Katona-sima, subsequently called "Porpoise Sound." A rock awash lies 3 or 4 hundred yards SE from the southern point of entrance. We steered NW about a mile, when the sound narrowed to less than half a mile width, and bent more to the westward. In this strait we found 6¾ fathoms water; and anchored. In a few minutes we found that a strong inflowing tide had drifted us off the shoal, and the soundings showed 28 fathoms. Sail was again made on the schooner, and at dark we anchored in a bay on the northern shore, about 2 miles beyond, in 9¾ fathoms water. There we saw a large village, and a junk secured to the beach. Shortly after coming to, a boat from the Vincennes,

[40] These islands lie between Great Liu Ch'iu [Ōkinawa] and Ōshima.

in charge of Lt. Fillebrown, came along side, with orders to join you near the western opening of the sound.

In the evening we visited the village abreast of us and found the beach spread with mats for our reception, with tea, saké and pipes. The dress of the people was Loo-Chooan, our entertainers wearing the silver hair pin. At first they objected to our entering the village, but one by one the party strayed off without personal hinderance. Every house seemed deserted. Conchs that had been blown in annunciation of our visit, had, I presume, warned all women and small children, to fly into the bushes. Finally one of the "silver pins" invited us into his residence, presented us with more tea and pipes, and, at leaving, with a dozen eggs each, nicely strung in plaited straw.

The following morning, having previously angled from the schooner and two shore stations, we got underway and beat thro the sound. A thunder shower this morning interrupted for the first time the beautiful weather hitherto experienced, but it cleared off brightly. Our course through the sound was like an intrusion into fairy land. There were all the features of romantic summer scenery: mountains, hills and valleys, either wildly wooded or rich in cultivation, with promontories and bays, grey cliffs and green slopes, and here and there a picturesque islet. The contours of the heights and the curves of the shore were equally wavy and graceful; and not least in beauty was the sea—blue water, one long shining reach, sweeping into such deep recesses on either side that Nature seemed to have been at play in modelling harbors. In this view, however, the great depth was not a convenience. In midsound we found 40 fathoms, rarely less than 10 up to the very shores.

The faces of the cliffs, where exposed, show a composition of shale, with a large angle of dip to the westward. The mountain timber is principally pine. Besides the universal rice, we saw wheat and Indian corn, tobacco and many garden vegetables in cultivation. A large raspberry of sweet flavor was in great profusion.

Parting company on the 3d [of May], we retraced our way through the sound and anchored again in the bay where we first arrived, devoting the afternoon to measuring a base by sound, and in examining the shoal near the eastern opening. It is a wide ledge projecting from "South point" very nearly to the opposite shore. As close to the former as any vessel would be likely to go, we found not less than 5 fathoms. Deepening slowly to 6 and 7 fathoms in midpassage, it terminates abruptly in blue water, say three fourths of the way across. Over it the ebb tide was running eastward at the rate of 3 knots per hour.

The following morning we stood out of the sound, and commenced some examination of the passage between Katona-sima and the more southern neighboring islands. There were many rocks, but there appeared to be a sufficiently practicable channel. Lowering weather, with mist and rain, prevented a thorough reconnaissance. The wind shifted to NW, and we worked along the east coast of Ou-sima under easy sail during the night.

5th. Beat up in shore close to Sena, a port indicated on a Japanese chart, to which my attention had been called in your instructions. I saw only a small bight (a fair junk anchorage I presume) with a village. Its appearance did not, I believe, warrant delay, and I stood on.

6th. We were beating to the northward with the wind from NNE. We cut in a large rock lying about two miles off the NE cape of Ou-sima. At 6 p.m. passed two miles south of "Macedonian rock." On the 7th the wind hauled to SE. At daylight we made Cleopatra (an extinct volcano) and Tou-kara island. Passed between Toukara and the Sabine islets, and ran along the western side of the chain to which these belong as far as St. Francois Xavier of the French chart. Archimedes volcano was burning, a large white cloud over it, and wreathed cloudlets floating off in the blue hazy atmosphere.

8th, at 2 A.M. Julie island, a volcano, bore East. At 4 we hove to. At daybreak St. Claire island (or Kouro-sima) and the Trio rocks were about 5 miles equidistant from us. We had also in sight, the high peaks of Motomi-yama on Jakuno-sima, Julie island smoking, Is. du Volcan (or Jiwo-sima) half veiled in its own vapors, and the small island of Apollos (or Tako-sima). It was superb, thus sailing along, to make these volcanic islands—mountains pass, as it were, in review, grouped yet solitary, each with its basaltic bluffs, wooded acclivities and lofty crater-cones; rising out of deep blue sea as from a plain.[41]

During the morning we saw many fishing boats. We stood into a small bay on the NE side of St. Claire seeking for anchorage, but, finding no bottom with 22 fathoms of line within one fourth of a mile of the shingle beach, tacked and stood off again. There was a village here, with many canoes. We passed along the northern shore of St. Claire, and then steered for Ingersoll rocks. Rounded these within half a mile, and steered to the Nd and Ed. The latitude and longitude of St. Claire and of these rocks we succeeded in finding with great accuracy; which was the more fortunate as a hazy horizon had prevented our fixing St. Claire with reference to Peak Horner. Passed two and a half miles to the eastward of de la Roche Poncié islands; and at 5 P.M., sighted Dobbin's rocks, the Symplegades and the Kosiki islands. The wind was fresh in puffs from SE, a cross chop sea making wet weather for us. Hove to for the night, head to the southd.[42]

On the 9th thick cloudy weather, with fresh winds from SE. During the night a northerly current had brought Cape Fajesaki to bear East. At 10 A.M., Stood into a deep, narrow

[41] These islands all lie between Ōshima and Tanegashima, and thus are strung between the Liu Ch'ius and southern Kyūshū.

[42] The *Fenimore Cooper* was now moving up the western coast of Kyūshū. She passed not far from Nagasaki on her way, charting islands in the direction of the straits which divide Kyūshū and Honshū from Korea.

bay immediately north of this cape. The water was green and waveless as a pond under its lee, but squalls more sudden and transient than the Magellan "williwaws," indicated by snow-white foam and whirls of smokey spray, were very frequent and violent: They are, I imagine, altogether similar to those described on your Ou-sima chart. We found no bottom with 30 fathoms line, and, failing to get anchorage, stood close along shore 5 miles, as far as a remarkable pillar rock; whose composition, as well as that of all the cliffs and isolated rocky towers and pinnacles, is a fine formation of gray columnar basalt. We passed several small coves with villages in them, the beaches sand and shingle. About a mile north of us, when we hauled off shore, was a line of large black rocks, stretching out about ½ a mile from a cape. Then, standing off until out of the sweep of whirlwinds from the ravines, we hove to, head to the Sd and Wd.

We were three days in all reconnoitering the western and northern shores of the Kosiki islands. In the published account of Admiral Krusenstern's voyages, this distinguished hydrographer has reported "a shelf rising from a group of black pointed rocks (Lat. 31° 42′ 20″ N. Long. 230° 26′ 30″ W.) 7 miles NW 39° from the SW Point Meac-sima" (or Simono-Kosiki) "seen a little before dark." He called them after the name of his ship. On the "Cecille" chart the Nadiejda rocks are drawn as islets, and lie seven miles nearly *north* of "the SW point of Meac-sima." On [J. Ph. Fr.] von Siebold's chart they lie seven miles N by W from the same point, and appear as small rocks. We must have passed exceedingly close to every one of these positions, yet we saw nothing of the rocks. Surprised at this, even allowing for the thick weather during part of the time, I concluded that they must be of the number of rocks which lie nearer in shore. Krusenstern's volume was not then in my possession, or I should have made the search in and about his position a conclusive one. Doubtless they exist, and it is to be presumed, however strangely we

[76]

missed them, that the bearing and distance so positively given by their discoverer are not far from the truth.

The Kosikis are a group of islands & islets, extending about 25 miles NE and SW, with winding channels between. A chain of high rocks stretches eastward full four miles from the east cape of the northern island (Kamino Kosiki) which narrows the space between the group and the coast of Kiusiu to about ten miles. The islands are various in elevation, area and conformation, and are very beautiful, in all the picturesqueness of trap rock, whose bold mountain fronts are again varied with softer hills, wood-crested and incurve symmetrical as a lady's eyebrows. The Japanese population seems to be large, and over all are clustering villages and a rich cultivation.

On the 11th we left the Kosikis, edged in a little towards the coasts of Kiusiu and Amakousa, and then steered for Cape Nomo. Every peak and point for a great distance was beautifully distinct during the day. On the 12th we had thick SE weather. Waiting for observations, we anchored 2 miles S by E ½ E from Cape Nomo, in 39 fathoms water, on a bottom of rocks and black sand. It rained heavily with rolling thunder. I commenced observations for current, and, at 4 P.M., took advantage of a temporary dispersion of the mists to secure time sights and a round of angles. Taka-sima and the Mitsusi rocks where open to the westward of the cape. The hills on the cape and on its adjacent islet of Kaba-sima appeared high and peaked, and crested with tall plumy trees like marching soldiers in Indian file. At dark the rain recommenced, with vivid sheet lightening and thunder, and the sea in fiery phosphorescence; and, at 11 P.M., up to which time it had been nearly calm, a fresh and very dirty squall from the Southd blew right on shore. We set reefed sails, weighed the kedge, and hove to at a safe offing; making allowance for the current to drift us, as it did, past the Mitsusi rocks and other dangers into the Goto Straits.

Until the 24th our work struggled on through many

impediments; through blinding rain-squalls, freshest from SE, but blown backwards and forwards from all points of the compass, fogs that wrapped us up as in a blanket, and the wearisome inactivity of calms—calms so utterly breezeless, that the water lay dead, and smooth, and shining, like oil, and was reticulated all over with fine films of the gossamer. In fifteen days we obtained but three latitudes, one only at meridian, and there were but two days in which we could observe the sun at pleasure.

Nevertheless, by patient industry and watchfullness, we were enabled to connect our reconnaisance of the coast as far as the north-west point of Kiusiu. The islands and rocks in the Goto Straits, and those situated inside of Iki island, were triangulated and closely examined, the main shore lines and mountains approximately determined. The schooner's first position was 3½ miles south of Firasima, being anchored in 17 fathoms, green water and sandy bottom. Shore stations were occupied, a base of four miles measured by sound, and then we moved on slowly from anchorage to anchorage, obtaining a longer base astronomically. In these narrow straits and passages we made the tides and currents of avail to us— indeed they were too often our only means of locomotion. The handiness of our little boat chain, in room of a hawser, we had many occasions to prove.

The whole western shore of Kiusiu is mountainous, so also are the Goto islands. The geological formation is volcanic. The soil of all the islands, large and small, is apparently very fertile; the summits timbered, the declivities cultivated in terraces. In the Goto Straits, so far as we observed, were no especial dangers for daylight navigation. I am pretty certain that we located every rock and reef in the narrower part of these straits. In only one place, that is some three miles due south of Jennisima, did we see any rocks covered at half tide; and these are in series with others more apparent. I would recommend the channel east of Ferasima, keeping rather close to that island. It has a clear look through the straits north and

[78]

south; you give all rocks an ample berth; and you can anchor at need in a convenient depth on sufficiently good holding ground.

Four noblemen or gentlemen came on board from Firasima. They were well dressed, with red and yellow silk capes, wore two swords each, and had a considerable retinue. The chief personage saluted me by touching the deck with his knees and fingers. I showed them my letter in Chinese, which stated the object and character of the vessel and of the expedition. Contrary to my expectation they gave us no intimation to leave.[43]

On a rock two miles south of Jennisima, about thirty feet high and covering perhaps an acre, I found no less than 60 or 70 fishermen, men and boys. When we first approached in the boat, the patriach [sic] of the party held up his hands, beseeching us, as I conceived, not to land; and, as a rock 200 yards distant offered the advantage of not being incommoded by the crowd, I pulled there and got my angles. After a timidity of about an hour, the whole concourse came over to us, were very polite and very inquisitive, and invited me over to the house which crowns, like a crow's nest, their little rock of habitation. Upon finishing my work I went there. The old chief gave me tea and a pipe, some dried fish and preserved sea-weed; and, in parting there was an impressive pantomimical supplication that, for my own sake, I would go south again. I asked him on board by gestures, in which he answered that he would lose his head. For many minutes, as we pulled away, they all waved us adieu.

The fishermen in the boats scattered through the straits, generally motioned us southward with almost frantic gesticu-

[43] The island of Hirado (at this time called Firando or Firasima by European navigators) contained the site on which the Portuguese and later the Dutch and English traded in the sixteenth century and until the Exclusion Edict of 1638. The nobles who visited the *Fenimore Cooper* must have been from the fief of Hizen, which included Hirado. The daimiates of Hizen and its neighbor to the south, Satsuma, were at this time more interested in foreign relations than most of the other principalities.

lation. Possibly they only referred to Nangasaki lying in that direction.

The rocks here are Amygdaloidal.

The island of Iki is not mountainous. It has gently undulating hills, with dark groves and groups of trees; and bright green slopes and terraces of cultivation, resembling some great prince's pleasure grounds of park and lawn—altogether a very beautiful island, and densely populated.

Long low islets and ledges of rocks extend from its southern and its eastern points. It abounds in bays and ports. Between it and Firato to the southward and Kiusiu to the eastward is quite an archipelago, of which there is no trace on Von Siebold's chart. Two high rocks, which I called Pisa Tower and Tent Rock, described by their titles, are remarkable objects. The average of our soundings in these straits was 30 fathoms, over a bottom of sand, coral and shells. The main Japanese coast is both mountainous and fertile, the conical form prevailing in the hills.

May 20th, we passed close inside of the ledges off the east cape of Iki, within 50 yards, the least water five fathoms, sandy bottom. There was a fresh breeze from the eastward, and thick rainy weather. Sailed round the north side of Iki, and when off the NW cape, saw what seemed to be a pretty little harbor, and heard two guns. We hauled by the wind, and stood in, firing our gun as we approached. The entrance is not more than 150 yards wide between a cliff of columnar basalt and some low rocks. Carried 5 fathoms water through it. We anchored in 4¼ fathoms (passing, however, over 3¼) and found the harbor to be formed by two small islands, a passage to the northward through which we came in, and one to the westward much wider; the space between the eastern island and mainland of Ikisima being closed in by rocks. The port is of small extent, but the town is large with many handsome white houses. On a hill of the western island was a lookout station with many flags, and they fired from it two more guns as we entered. No sooner had we anchored than 53 boats, each averaging 20 sitters, men women and children, babes in arm included, came alongside, and our visitors *piled* on board—that is the men did, the women contenting themselves with coming close under the quarter. The men were mostly in the most primitive of costumes, the women wore very little more clothing, but manifested the universal feminine desire for ornament in head dresses of flowers or gay-colored handkerchiefs. Some were rather good looking, but the majority were repulsive with their painted crimson lips and blackened teeth. Men and women were alike eager for navy buttons and trifles in general. In a little while several guard boats came alongside, and did us some service in ordering the crowd off, which had become rather troublesome. They hung round us pertinaciously, however, until sunset, when I shoved them off, guard boats and all. I had asked for water, poultry, vegetables and eggs. At dark they sent us off about 100 gallons of the former, and promised to send us the other articles the next day. As we sailed at daylight, I did not give them time either to fulfil or break their promise.

Shortly after we anchored (it was raining) about a dozen soldiers, six of them with matchlocks, came to the beach abreast of the schooner, on the side opposite the town, and ranged themselves seated; the soldiers with straw rain jackets on, the matchlocks covered. They displayed two tri-colored flags, with three round moons in each field; the same insignia being on the flags, hats and capes of the soldiers in the guard boats.[44] I caused the arms to be loaded, to be prepared for accident; and sent on shore for the commanding officer or someone in authority to come off, in order to explain to him what we were, and to demand the withdrawal of this menacing squad. No one came; but the military party almost immediately dispersed, or rather disappeared.

The next morning, but not until we were well out of the

---

[44] Doubtless these were samurai wearing the mōn, or crest, of the Sō family, which ruled the daimiate from the Tsushima, not far from Ikishima.

port, the tri-colored and tri-mooned banners were again displayed over a similar martial array.

I lingered in the Straits of Krusenstern until the morning of the 24th, vainly watching in the midst of fog and rain to secure sights properly to determine the northern capes of Iki and the southern ones of Tsus-sima. Our time growing short, and much work remaining to be done, I reluctantly bore up for Colnett's island. We succeeded in fixing it very well, though the atmosphere was too hazy to see any other land. The island is high and rounded.[45]

On the 25th was a lovely day, with SW breezes. We passed close to Mi-sima, making a large correction in its position, and followed along the coast of Niphon in its curve from eastern to northern trend in near reconnaissance. We saw one or two fine bays, green coast hills, and a long lofty range of mountains inland. Numerous fishing boats around us.

26th. We coasted northward as far as Cape Fisami-saki, where the land bends again to the eastward, and steered NNE for the Oki islands, heaving to near them for the night. We passed many incurvatures and apparent ports. The immediate shores were rather low, with occasional ribands of sand beach; then rose a range of high coast hills, greenly wooded, with reddish cliffs, and mountains in ascending scale. Each mountain is remarkable for its height, isolation, proximity to the coast, and its table summit; and we got many cuts on it, and measured its altitude. As a general thing, we have data for the heights of all prominent peaks, headlands and islands during our coasting voyage.

The water was blue all day until past Fisami-saki, when it became green.

We saw numerous junks, some of considerable size. The

[45] Acting Lieutenant Gibson was now taking the schooner between Korea and western Japan. Krusenstern Strait is now known by its Japanese name, Tsushima Strait. It was here that the famous naval battle between the Russian Grand Fleet and the Japanese Imperial Fleet was fought in 1905.

Soon the *Fenimore Cooper* was cruising northeastward along the western coast of Honshū (Niphon), the central Japanese island.

Japanese sailors sometimes shouted at us, sometimes laughed, and always stared with intense curiosity.

It was showery, but not misty, during this day, and the one ensuing, in which we reconnoitred the islands of Oki.

There are four principal islands in this group, hilly and green, a number of islets and a few rocks off the points. I wished to pass between the islands, there being plainly a wide safe channel, but baffling airs and currents preventing our approach nearer than six miles to the eastern side of the group. We noticed several harbor-like bights.

On the 28th a fine breeze and beautiful weather. Being so pressed for time, I did not like to deflect any to the southward, and steered due East, to verify the general trend of the coast abreast of us and come up with it again where it bends to the northward. We saw it bearing from SSE to SW, say 35 miles distant, trending about E by N and W by S.

29th stood in for the land on the west side of the peninsula of Noto, and followed it up at distances varying from 2 to 5 miles. The water was green and soundings rather shoal. A sandy ridge, from 50 to 100 feet high, forms the seashore. It is dotted with trees and bushes. Then there expands a wide plain, ornamented with groves and verdant fields. This plain is intersected with creeks, the openings of several of which we saw. Then the mountains rise up, step by step, until they reach the "unascended majesty" of three great snowy peaks.

As we proceeded northward, the shore rose into hills, more like the land further south, and we lost sight of the snow mountains. We got good observations during the day, time sights by the moon and Venus in the evening, and a meridian altitude of the moon. At 6 p.m. passed Cape Noto, made the Astrolabe islets, and hove to for the night.

These islets are barren rocks. We reconnoitred them in the morning, and bore up for the island of Jootsima, 15 miles to the northward of them. Jootsima is a great deal further west than its assigned Longitude. The whole coast, as drawn on Siebold's chart, is too far east. So also are the tabled longitudes in Raper. Latitudes in many instances we have found very incorrect.

Jootsima is very low, flat, bushy, covered with houses, and lined with reefs, with hundreds of fishing boats. It is dangerously situated for navigation, all the more for its little height. At night a vessel would be on it before it could be seen.

May 31st and the 1st June examined the northern side of the peninsula of Noto and the large island of Sado. The northern half of Sado is mountainous, with yellowish precipices which resemble patches of snow; the southern half of the island is much lower. There is a very deep bay on either side (eastern and western) and numerous smaller bights, with villages and flotillas. About twenty boats filled with the inhabitants came off to visit us. Soon the guard boats came, the soldiers first making a sketch of the schooner, and afterwards they ordered the people away, whose curiosity, however, seemed almost to overcome their awe of authority. We saw no women, one little girl only. The soldiers wore one sword, silk jackets and lackered umbrella-shaped hats. The common people were clothed in coarse cotton, sometimes in nothing at all. One of the most respectable looking individuals, not a soldier, asked in the Chinese character a few civil questions about the schooner, and offered to pilot us into the port whence he came, then about two miles distant. Another, a venerable old man, gave me, with quite an air, one piece of cash carefully enveloped, and a small piece of silk braid. I gave him a lead pencil in return, which delighted him exceedingly. All the faces around us, even those of the soldiers (stoical in trying to conquer the invincible curiosity which yet looked out of their eyes) were smiling and friendly. When the guard boats left, some of the other boats returned, and a few followed us five or six miles.

June 2d. On this morning, as on one or two previous occasions, we found that a fall in the barometer had resulted in no change of weather. It was fine. At 9 P.M. we were three miles north of Awa-sima, having cut in this island, many tangents of Sado, and peaks and points on Niphon. A conspicuous snow mountain, which I subsequently called Mount Pierce, was angled on all day. Awa-sima is hilly, but low and small, and is about ten miles from the mainland.

3d. Passed 6 or 7 miles west of Tobi-sima which is small and low, and covered with bushes. There is a detached bushy islet to the southward of it, and some rocks. Mount Pierce is not crowned with snow, but has quantities of it in its unsunned hollows and ravines. Rising not far from the coast, it is prominent from many views, and in its sloping pyramidal form, and rosy whiteness at long distances, is beautiful to see. Between it and the Cape of the Russians further north are three deep bays, besides the inlet under the latter promontory.

We passed the Cape of the Russians within three miles, and Cape Gamaley within ½ a mile. Close to the latter we lost the fresh SE breeze we had carried all day.

The Cape of the Russians is a high mountain, with long declivities (radii like the crimps of a ruff) which terminate in bluffs; and its connection with the main land of Niphon being a low isthmus, it has every appearance of an island. So it is called on the chart—*Wasika-sima*; but the tracing of the shore line contradicts the name, and makes it a peninsular promontory. It is timbered, but not thickly. The points are rocky; and off the northern extremity of the cape is a separate reef half a mile long, its outer rock more than a mile from shore.

Between this remarkable promontory and a point of high land south of Cape Gamaley, is a very deep bay. Under Cape Gamaley itself is a large bight, apparently well sheltered; but, though close to it in passing, it was too late in the evening to examine it. Indeed I have to regret that want of time prevented our surveying many inviting harbors, which we passed on all portions of the coast.

The shore in view this day was as a general thing hilly, except the isthmus at the Cape of the Russians. There were many mountain ranges inland, and three snow peaks to the southward of Mount Pierce. The minor features of the scenery were as usual charming.

The highlands of Cape Gamaley are not dissimilar to those of the Cape of the Russians, showing a central summit and out sloping points. The western point of this promontory, however, stretches further out in low land than the others, being a smooth green hill, with a green islet close to it.

June 4th. The weather had entirely changed. We had fresh squalls from the Eastward, and at 10 a.m. quite a gale. The schooner was put under close reefed foresail, and hove to, or run as she appeared to drift towards any of the land that lay all around us, and that loomed occasionally through the mist. We got glimpses of the high mountains on Jesso [Ezo, Yezo, or Hokkaidō], the coast of Niphon near Capes Greig and Sangar, and the island of Kosima. A strong current to the eastward, with occasional violent ripplings, but no swells.

5th. Fanned with light airs, assisted by the current, into the Straits of Sangar [Tsūgarū]; and at 3 p.m. made the promontory of Hakodadi.

Cape Greig is a bold headland, with red rocky bluffs, and ragged peaks. Peak Tilesius, spoken of by Admiral Krusenstern as so remarkable a mountain, I did not see, owing to the thick weather. The entrance to the Straits of Sangar is strongly marked by the off-lying volcanic islands (one only of which we saw), the mountain cape of Nadiejda on Jesso, with its fringe of rocks, and the long slope and abrupt termination of Cape Sangar. Close to the latter cape is a small peaked islet, or, more properly, a large rock.

The thick weather and rapid currents stopped our running survey from the time of making these straits. Our sights for latitude and longitude were indifferent, and the angles we took not very accurate. I therefore consider our reconnaissance as terminating at Cape Gamaley.[46]

[46] These names of places in northern Honshū (Niphon) are now out of usage. They may be found on the second map, entitled "Chart of the Coast of China and of the Japan Islands . . ." appended to the work: *Narrative of the Expedition of An American Squadron to the China Seas and Japan . . . Under the*

In the absence of a draughtsman and there being but one officer with me, having been actively employed all the while, nearly all of our work remains unplotted. This report is submitted simply as a narrative and series of general descriptions, and contains little of precise hydrographical detail.

Acting Lieutenant [Beverley] Kennon's sights and computations, compared with one another, or tested by the relative positions of objects, have been accurate to a nicety almost beyond precedent. I cannot too warmly express my satisfaction.

A mean back rate for the chronometers has to be applied to the determinations at the times of observation. A table of latitudes and longitudes, thus corrected, is in preparation.

I have the honor to be, Sir,

Very respectfully,
Your Obdt. Servt.

Lieutenant John Rodgers,   WILLIAM GIBSON
Commanding U.S. Surveying Expedn. Actg. Lieut. Comdg.
to the North Pacific, &c.
Ship Vincennes

U.S. Ship Vincennes
Port of Hakodadi
June 22d, 1855

[Commander John Rodgers]
Sir:

In accordance with your instructions I have, in the launch of the Vincennes, examined and partially surveyed 450 miles of the Eastern Coast of the Island of Nippon, from Simoda to Hakodadi, and shall at the earliest moment present a full report of the voyage to which this is preliminary.

Sailing from Simoda on the 28th May, we encountered headwinds, rain and a rough sea, the land was obscured. In

Command of Commodore M. C. Perry . . . , vol. II. Washington, A. O. P. Nicholson, 1856.

[87]

the evening we anchored in a small boat harbor (Sino Hama) ten or twelve miles north of Simoda; there a portion of our crew slept upon the shore. Information of our arrival reaching Simoda, and interpreters from that place boarded us at dawn. They were told that we were going from Simoda to Hakadodi, that the weather was bad and we had anchored for the night; that as it had become favorable we would depart. They offered to supply us with fresh provisions, and the offer was accepted: there was an apparent design to delay us, we therefore sailed.

The north wind continuing, we stood toward the volcanic Island of Oho-Sima. At noon we found a powerful current sweeping us to the North and East. A South wind sprang up and in company with thirty large junks from Seaward, we ran towards the entrance of the Bay of Jedo [Edo], in order to connect the running Survey of the Coast of Nippon with the observations made at Simoda, by triangulation upon prominent peaks of the mountain ranges. Our boat spreading much canvass, easily passed the vessels of the Japanese, though before the wind they sail well. It seemed as we came up that they endeavored to keep aloof, we approached them to within a cables length. At evening there were few ahead. Coming into the wake of the largest we followed her towards the Bay of Jedo; at sunset its entrance was in sight, we then hauled off intending to anchor under Cape Susaki, but the wind heading us from the East we anchored North of the larger of two islands shown in Siebolds chart. Near it and outside of us was a large fleet of boats, perhaps an hundred, probably fishermen; they did not perceive us. At first supposing them to be guard boats we edged away to the North in passing and prepared our arms.

In the morning they were gone and we examined the Bay of Susaki, which is capacious with good holding ground and easy of access, open to the West but more safe than the port of Simoda. It is near the entrance to the Bay of Jedo. Upon the extremity of Cape Susaki is a work of eight embrasures.[47]

[47] A navigational chart of the Bay of Susaki was made by this venturesome crew and was included in the first volume of the expedition's correspondence.

Running to the East we attempted unsuccessfully to weather Cape King. At night found shelter in a rocky basin frequented by fishermen and adjoining a shallow bay formed by a reef, and in which were moored several small junks: a village named Sino Hama, literally white beach, stood upon the shore, and a temple upon the promontory separating the two harbors. The inhabitants to the number of five or six hundred covered the sides of the basin in which we were lying and so dense was the throng that we could with difficulty find a footing upon the shore. We landed and walked a short distance into the country, entered their houses and were kindly received. The harvest was being gathered in and the heaps of yellow grain gave an agricultural air of plenty to the place. The young men are employed in fishing and the females manage the farms, usually of small extent. There were but three sword wearing officials seen and they did not appear to be inclined to limit our rambles or our intercourse with the people. At night we slept in the boat but before the dawn were awakened by the voices of our friends, who at that early hour resumed their stations upon the rocks. There were men women and children, many of the latter at the breast. So inquisitive were these people that we and our apparel were subjected to the closest scrutiny; indeed, the beats of our pulses were numbered, the temperature of our hands tried. Nor were the females less forward than the men in these investigations; it seemed that they would not have hesitated to admit us as members of their families. The young girls were engaging in their manners and some of them were singularly beautiful: but the married women were disfigured in our estimation by the blackening of their teeth to which we were not yet accustomed.

At this port we first saw a portion of the fishing fleet engaged off the SE extremity of Nippon where the Sea affords abundance. Their large boats, double the length of our launch, were propelled with great velocity by twelve men, and in the management of their powerful sculling oars they exhibit the most perfect specimens of athletic and graceful men that I have ever seen. A single stripe of cloth about their loins left to view their fine persons, and in leaving the port many of them threw into their action an air of pride.

Leaving this hospitable port we rounded Cape King and entered the bight upon which Siebold places several villages and anchorages. As the evening approached we sought in vain for some shelter, two villages were visited in succession but the ports were hardly worthy of the name, for a few rocks breaking the rollers permitted their flat and light boats by dexterous management to land upon the beach where they were hauled beyond the reach of the waves.

The barometer slowly falling and clouds forming to the S West it was thought expedient to leave the lee land for the open sea.

As we stood out, a sea without warning broke with great violence near the boat, but only once, rain fell and fitful gusts swept over us. In the morning standing in to examine a port which appeared little better than those seen the preceding evening, we were overhauled by eighty fishing boats, manned by more than a thousand men; the press was tremendous and to avoid carrying away our jib boom it was rigged in. We were upon our guard, but from these unceremonious people we experienced only kindness; they threw into our boat fish of various species, rice, tobacco and wood; each boat thus offered a tribute which was always accepted, returning them fishing hooks, lead, buttons &c. Finally we were so hemmed in that we lost steerage way and got out our oars upon which they made more room for us, but still heedless of our remonstrances pressing by us and ahead we intimated our desires more clearly by discharging a revolver athwart their bows, which they took in good part and laughing left us to pursue our course.

It became necessary to replenish our water barecas and we therefore entered a deep but small bay, formed by a reef, bare at low water, upon which were some hundreds of the Japanese collecting sea weed apparently for exportation; three large junks were lying in the harbor which opens to the South and is not inviting to ships of large size. We were visited by officials and supplied with wood and water; remuneration was declined and no persuasion induced them to receive it. We were permitted to land but not to visit the town. There is a spring of excellent water, at the foot of a verdant hill surmounted by a temple, and within a stone cast of the anchorage. We left an hour or two after anchoring, examining the most important portions of the bay and its entrance. In accomplishing the survey we employed our oars, and the weather cloth being down, the rollers at the entrance of the harbor rendered the operation somewhat hazardous.

On the 3rd June having laid off the land during the night, there being no harbors south of Daiho Saki, we were off that cape. There are towns upon its south & north shores; the former are fishing hamlets with unprotected beaches, the latter has apparently a fine harbor formed by a reef in the North bight of the Cape, and is of considerable importance. Several junks were lying within the reef, its entrance is towards the extremity of the Cape and is well defined: if there is sufficient water the inner harbor would be a very desirable one for ships in distress. The Cape itself protects an anchorage possessing good holding ground, open only towards the North, soundings regular. The town would doubtless afford supplies of wood, water and provisions. We regretted exceedingly that time could not be devoted to a close examination of this port; head winds and adverse currents had delayed us much and they seemed to prevail. There was a long line of coast before us without harbors; and as it was indispensable that the launch should not retard the ship from sailing on her voyage, at the only available season, to examine Behring Straits, we reluctantly left this inviting harbor, its town glittering white in the sun. Subsequently we found that the difficulties in our way had not been over-rated.

On the 4th of June the wind came out ahead with rain and

fog, we were nearly up with Cape Kennis [Konasaki], the
barometer fell and the swell from SE increased very much,
until the waves ran high as our boats mast-head. The sound
of the breakers was distinctly heard. At 3 P.M. the weather
was very threatening and we bore up for deeper water to the
SE and a position whence, if a heavy gale set in, we might
make the port of Daiho-saki eighty miles to leeward. The
rollers had not yet broken though the NE wind had raised a
sea of its own. The square sail and whole mainsail were set,
and we then had an opportunity of admiring the good quali-
ties of our boat; with her true gunwale often eighteen inches
below the water, and her cloth to its edge, she yet answered
her helm and attained a surprising swiftness. We desired to
leave the rollers, over which we sailed as over hills, before
they should break, when the safety of even a larger vessel
would become doubtful. We were rapidly clearing the land
when a sea was observed to break about two points on our
weather bow, a column of white foam high in the air. The
helm put down, the sails lowered and the main quickly reefed
to weather it, we were relieved in seeing the jet of a spouting
whale in the hollow of the sea: it was upon his back that the
sea had broken and not upon a rock.

So admirably did the boat head the waves which now began
to curl, that we laid her by the wind under balanced reefed
mainsail and foresail for the night. There were indications of
Cirro cumuli in the haze of the sky, the sun broke faintly
through and at midnight the clouds were going, the moon
was up, the sea moderating, and a cast of the lead gave thirty-
nine fathoms.

We were pleased indeed, for the rain had drenched us and
we were chilled by the N East wind.

On the 7th. We had made but little progress although oars
had been used when practicable. From Daiho Saki to the Bay
of Sendai there are no harbors. On the evening of the 8th we
had a fresh wind and heavy sea and stood out from the land;
in the morning saw the high land about the Bay of Sendai.

That evening a North-Easter came on, the rain poured incessantly, a thick mist shut out the land. A lee shore and no shelter, we were again forced to carry sail to get an offing. In the early night a remarkably luminous sea beneath a black and lowering sky presented an impressive scene; but the wind hauled to the N West and on the morning of the 9th we were off the Bay of Sendai and saw the great Mountains inland capped with snow, the weather cleared and the sun came out. We were charmed with this magnificent bay: It affords numerous harbors, and according to the season of the year one may be preferred to another, but there are some entirely protected. Crossing a bar, upon which the water broke at one fathom, we entered the river Tomigawa, to the town of Isokona. The river is about two hundred yards wide and from one to three fathoms deep. A rapid ebb running as we came in, fourteen large junks lay moored before the town. Between four and five thousand persons of both sexes assembled upon the shore, their eyes were fixed upon us: it was not pleasant to be so intensely gazed at by so many people. We were within ten yards of the shore, we wanted wood and water, they seemed to be satisfied in gazing, there was not a breath of air, perfect silence reigned upon the river. A letter was waved to them, messengers were seen to detach themselves from the throng and to run. In a few moments a number of officers arrived, they came on board [and] were agitated and trembled excessively. We endeavored to put them at their ease and soon succeeded. All the boats of the river were then launched and overburdened, thronged round us, some filled with water drenching their occupants, men were falling overboard in every direction, and the people on shore waded out into the river to see us more closely: even some who were blind faced the boat intently for hours. I do not believe that any European has entered this river.

The object of our voyage was explained to the officials by a letter in the Chinese character, they were informed of our wants, which were immediately supplied. We understood from them that it was necessary to communicate with the Prince or the Ruler of the district before they could supply us with more than provision for the day, and that as he resided at a considerable distance, three days would be required for the answer. They brought us boiled rice and tea from the fire; they gave us all the wood we asked for, and offered to bring spring water if we preferred it to that of the river, privately they gave us fresh eggs and vegetables, but were studious of concealment. They declined permitting me to walk in the town. Our gilded buttons were objects of admiration and they received them readily.

Many police officers wearing tassels of red silk, and devices upon their loose coats, surrounded the boat, they carried light wands and used them upon their forward countrymen, one of whom while examining a pistol, shown him by a seaman, suddenly cocked it and pulled the trigger, firing it. The guards instantly seized the unfortunate offender, he was thrown down and with a companion bound hand & foot, most painfully. I interceded for them and the principal visitor promised to represent the matter to the authorities. The intercession seemed pleasing to the Japanese, with the exception of the police who were tenacious of their priviliges.

The tide low and the sea breaking on the bar, it was thought imprudent to attempt the passage, we therefore dropped down to a more quiet anchorage. A guard boat accompanied us, at a late hour boats carrying lanterns were seen approaching, they contained the officials who questioning us upon the subject of our desires, as to the character of the food we required; and again gave us to understand that in three days an answer would be received from the Chief of the district, and that then, anything could be freely given us, they then left us and were followed by the guard boat. We were however not suffered to repose in quiet, for several boats filled with men and women came alongside; they offered their pipes and tobacco and conversed with us by signs. In the morning we got under way and pulled out over the bar, but not until we had received a morning call from the officials and another meal of rice and tea. They wished us to remain longer, but finding that we could not be persuaded, landed and the Standard bearer running to the seashore waved his flag in the direction of the deepest water of the bar, inclining its staff to the right or left thus indicating the course.

Before leaving the bay it was deemed prudent to land on some secluded spot and to cook the remaining salt provision, and it was desirable that the crew confined for so long a time should have exercise on shore. We landed on a small island clothed with cedars and other trees; fires were made and at noon we were ready to proceed. Many boats came loaded with visitors, from them we procured fish and shells. As we took our departure the officers of Isokona were seen approaching, we passed them and stood out, several boats following us. A number of fishermen who had been successful in their employment pulled rapidly to us holding up to view fine large fish which they freely gave us. Meanwhile dark clouds formed over the land and thunder began to roll among the mountains, a squall passed and rain fell. A large boat bearing a standard came to us and an officer whom we had not before seen, invited us to anchor in an arm of the bay close by. We accepted the invitation. The official, who seemed more a landsman than a sailor, offered to tow us in, and to test his sincerity we gave him a line, which he took and began in earnest to tow us. Manning our oars, his crew were forced to direct their efforts to keeping ahead of us, rather than to towing. They thought it a pleasing jest and laughed good humoredly. The anchorage to which, accompanied by twenty boats, we were thus conducted, proved to be a good one and adapted to the largest vessels. We were most kindly received by the inhabitants who gave us various trifles of personal ornament as tokens of their good will and friendship. We were surprised by the reappearance of the Isokona officials; they brought radishes, turnip tops and eggs, to me they presented a box of confectionary, a fan, and a little box, to which I made a suitable return. Late in the evening another supply of rice & tea was brought to us, and our crew seemed to think they were in polit[e]ness bound to return Captain Rice as they facetiously termed our Caterer empty platters.

We found a plentiful supply of fresh water on the beach, a rivulet runs there.

At daylight on the 11th we weighed and accompanied by numerous boats stood out to sea. The Isokona officials came after us in hot pursuit, and we luffed to the wind for them. The chief by word and gesture pressed us to return, he seemed to entertain a real affection for us, told us that if we would delay our departure the Governor or prince would visit us, that he was coming, and that we should have all the luxuries that the land afforded; And when at last I pointed to the open sea and gently put his hand aside, he stepped back into his boat and perfectly dejected regarded us with a longing look as we sailed away; and until beyond the range of vision we could see the motionless figure of Captain Rice. The kindness of this man made a deep impression upon our crew, and he was often the subject of conversation.

With a fair wind we coasted Northward surveying as we ran, but at night the wind hauled ahead and we stood in for an inviting bay containing several islands forming commodious harbors. Under one of them we anchored, visiting the habitations of a party of fishermen, who at first distrustful soon became familiar and cordial. In the morning we again ran out, but only to find light baffling airs from the NE. A powerful current set us twelve miles to the Southward during the night, although we made ... by log five to the Northward. Resorting to our oars we reached another bay where in a sheltered cove we anchored for the night.

In the morning we left, looking first into a splendid haven; but the weather was unfavorable, rain haze and NE wind. We sought refuge in another cove where an opportunity of drying our clothes was afforded by the furnace of a salt manufactory. The rain was constant and we had made so little progress that we became impatient. When we arrived the fishermen of the hamlet had just returned and a division of their fish was being made, they placed an equal share for our crew and gave them to us voluntarily.

On the morning of the 15th the sky was clear and a light air ruffled the sea. We hastened away and, a strong wind coming from the SE, we rapidly shortened the distance to our destined port. All night we pushed on carrying sail hard, and in the morning the bluff adjoining Cape Sinjosaki was in sight. We passed it and entered the Straits of Sangar. At ten P.M. we reached the anchorage of Hakodadi. We were 21 days on the passage.

With the exception of about 50 miles we have successfully made a running survey of the Coast. Data have been obtained for the determination of all prominent and important points. From Cape King to the Bay of Sendai there are no secure harbors, unless Daiho Saki may be so considered. North of that place the coast is low and appears to produce rice in abundance. Several junks were passed at anchor on the open coast. One from which we obtained a supply of wood was taking in a cargo of rice; their large flat boats are adapted to landing in surf. On that line of coast the soundings are regular, a constant swell prevails from S East, and near the land, in eight fathoms, is occasionally very heavy. From the Bay of Sendai to the Haven of Nanbu the coast is a series of harbors, the country well watered and wooded. The currents near the land generally set to the Southward. We obtained characteristic specimens of bottom for every section of the Coast.

The climate resembles that of our sea board about the same season of the year. N East winds bring rain and mist, the atmosphere becomes clear as the wind hauls to the NW or South. South West winds seldom blow, they change by the East or by the West without regularity. Usually South winds began at ten in the forenoon and the North as the sun set. When the winds changed during the day they generally hauled by the East but at night by the West. Northerly winds predominate.

From Simoda to Hakodadi there are neither outlying rocks nor shoals, and a ship may approach to within a mile of the shore without danger. We saw many of the whales known to whalemen as humped backs but neither sperm nor right whales. Nothing but the possibility of causing delay in the departure of the Vincennes from Hakodadi for the North, prevented a closer Survey of the Coast and its harbors.

The launch, though smaller than usual, carried with ease fifteen persons, provisions for fourteen days, an hundred and twenty gallons of water, one of Dahlgrens twelve pounder howitzers of 430 lbs., forty rounds of amunition, Carbines, cutlasses, pistols and pikes. She was well fitted. Her poop, forecastle and weather clothes enabled her to withstand seas which without those additions would have swamped her.

To Mr. [Edward M.] Kern, who accompanied Frémont on his explorations, and thus acquired experience and skills, I am indebted for the outlines of the land, illustrations, topographical sketches and valuable assistance. The launch's crew conducted themselves admirably at sea and in port. Mr. Berry sailmaker of the Vincennes also a volunteer, assisted materially in the prosecution of the work.

Very respectfully
Yr. obt Svt.

JOHN M. BROOKE
Actg. Liut
U.S. Navy

John Rodgers Esq.
Commanding U.S. Surveying Epetn.
to North Pacific &c.

Omitted from this account are various listings by longitude and latitude of islands situated between Hongkong and Kyūshū, also abstracts of the logs of the *Vincennes* and *John Hancock* from Hongkong to Hakodaté in 1855, as well as an abstracted log of the *Fenimore Cooper* from Naha to Hakodaté.

[Secretary Dobbin]

Sir!

I have the honor to enclose copies of the correspondence which I have had with the Governors of Hakodadi, and Simoda, in relation to certain American citizens who had come to Japan to reside temporarily.

It would occupy your time to no purpose were I to recapitulate the substance of the correspondence.

I have taken the ground which I deemed the government would wish taken.

I stated that I was not instructed in relation to the matter, but that in such cases, the Commanders of vessels of war, were required to write the interpretation they believed their government would give.

I have made the Japanese to understand that should my views be supported at home, my letter is sufficient notification of it.

It was expressly stated to me, that the Governor of Hakodadi was very sorry, we had his good wishes, but he could answer no otherwise than he has done. I replied, that I understood perfectly, it was as though I should receive orders to fire on Hakodadi, that I should be very sorry, that there are many good people in the city, but that I could not do otherwise than fire.

It was assented that the cases were similar. The Japanese government may I apprehend, endeavour to disavow the[ir] responsibility, should the United States press the question.

I sent my letter to the Governor of Simoda on May the 20th, there has been ample time for an answer.

It was understood in Simoda, that the citizens of the United States, passengers in the "Caroline Foote," had come to reside in Hakodadi under the treaty.

I do not think the positive refusal of the Japanese to accept the construction I believe the [United States] government has given to the treaty, and their positive refusal to wait for a joint construction, is to be regretted.

The treaty was not in my opinion made with any intention of abandoning the seclusion which has so long been the policy of their nation.

Every thing marks that they mean by not trading, to drive commerce away, and by not furnishing supplies, to induce ships to seek them elsewhere.

Trade was refused except for things of necessity. I obtained a copy of the treaty in Japanese, it is doubtless such as is furnished to the Officers for their governance.

Article 7th is not the same in the two languages. Article 7th in Japanese, is as I have been made to understand the following—

It is agreed, that Ships of the United States resorting to the ports open to them, shall be permitted to exchange gold, and silver, coin, and articles of goods, for other articles of goods, such as may be necessary for them, under such regulations, as shall be temporarily established by the Japanese government for that purpose.

It is stipulated, however, that the ships of the United States shall be permitted to carry away whatever articles they are unwilling to exchange.

"Such as may be necessary for them," is not in our published copy, and it alters the whole meaning of the article.

Whether this interpolation arose from fraud, I cannot say.

The Japanese have for ages kept their country secluded, they have refused permission for foreigners to learn their language. There is probably no American well versed in it. In future, we might properly refuse to sign a Japanese document. In the Dutch language, we should meet on common ground.

Should the government desire to do away with the evasions of the Japanese, the remedy must be held in the hands of the United States.

There are miles of waste land around Hakodadi, with a soil as fine apparently as any in the world.

The botanist, Mr. [Charles] Wright, who has roamed over Texas and other very fruitful soils, does not know where he could find better land than the waste plains here. We should hire the fields at a price fixed by ourselves, with liberty to cultivate them in our own manner, with Americans, or Japanese, or Chinese. Thus only can supplies for ships be ensured.

Custom Houses should be established with liberty on paying duties to take goods out of them, and do with them what we please, with the power of giving them away, or selling them to any Japanese without restriction.

No remedy occurs to me for a difficulty in obtaining return cargoes should the Japanese tell their merchants not to buy, nor exchange, they would not dare to do so.

The promulgation of a decree from the Emperor, permitting trade, printing and distributing the edict ourselves, with the promise of protecting the Japanese in the exercise of this law, might answer the end.[48]

Whatever the treaty may contain should be acted upon immediately, the land selected, and given in possession, goods entered, and traded at once, and houses advertised for, and lived in. Thus a precedent of what we mean, and of what they give, will be established before the force disperses. Afterwards, the Japanese cannot well retract, or pretend to have mistaken the meaning.

It could be easily explained that all this was to prevent misunderstanding of the treaty. We should have an express right to hire houses, or to build them, or to live at inns, as in other countries.

Should the government of the United States decide that the matter is serious enough for the employment of coercion, it would be humane to use a sufficient force at first. The Japa-

[48] Article Third of the Treaty of Yedo, July 29, 1858, provided almost exactly for what Commander Rodgers here suggested. See Hunter Miller (ed.), *Treaties and Other International Acts . . .* , VII, p. 952.

nese will be terrified, and overcome, without having received the petty injuries which irritate, and provoke resistance—leaving a resentment which prevents cordial good feeling afterwards.[49]

Osacka the great commercial emporium of Japan, cannot be approached very closely by large ships. Bomb launches of very light draught might be put together with screws, taken apart, placed on board the large steamers and set up in Japan. Boarding nettings would be necessary for them.

The Russian Admiral in Simoda gained his points by always threatening to go to Jedo. He would get up during the conference, and say, "Well gentlemen, we will talk of this matter no longer, I am going to Jedo"—he would then appear to leave. The Japanese would run after him, and say, "Stop, we may perhaps arrange it," and then upon further discussion, they gave way.

This hint may be of use. Where ever the vessels might rendezvous preparatory to the discussion of the treaty, whether here, or in Heda, or under Susaki Point, at the SE entrance of Jedo Bay (where the launch found good protection, and excellent holding ground of mud—), a revision of it would best take place off the palace at Jedo.

The American gentlemen who came to Japan to reside were told in Simoda, by the Russians, that the Emperor had ordered all the bells except two in each city to be sent to Jedo to be run into cannon. It is said that he has established the manufacture of arms in the capital, and made thousands after American models. One of the Japanese who has seen a good deal of foreigners stated to Purser Boggs that he knew we were stronger than they, but that the Emperor thought otherwise.

[49] In similar words Commodore Perry had argued for an impressive naval squadron to back up his diplomacy. Such frank utterances give the lie to the pre-Pearl Harbor occidental misimpression: that the reopening of Japan by Perry and others was conducted in such a way as to inspire confidence on the part of the Japanese. There were not lacking expressions of this sort by individual Japanese, but the basic feeling was a compound of perilous exposure, fear, and a determination to hold off the Westerners until protection could be devised.

These I give as rumours merely, and not as positively known, but they are worth repeating, and may explain what we should not otherwise understand.

With a very human weakness, it may be that the matters under my eyes seem far more important than they will do when viewed from a distance.

I beg you will except this excuse, should my letter appear intemperate.

I have the honor to be

Very Respectfully
Your obdt servt.

JOHN RODGERS
Comdg. U.S. Surveying Expedition
to the North Pacific Ocean, &c.

Honorable James C. Dobbin
Secretary of the Navy
Washington, D.C.

At Shimoda and Hakodaté, Commander Rodgers took up the cause of American merchants who desired to secure residences on shore so as to sell imports and to purchase fresh cargoes. The following correspondence, which was enclosed with dispatches to Washington, will indicate the nature of Japanese caution and of American arguments.

Yakushen Temple
Com. Rodgers,   Kakisaki, Japan
Commanding U.S. Exploring Expedition,   May 11th, 1855
Harbor of Simoda

Dear Sir!

We, the undersigned citizens of the United States of America, most respectfully beg leave to represent to you Sir, That on the publication of the American Treaty with Japan, we were lead to believe that in accordance with one, or more articles of said Treaty, Americans would be permitted to reside in Simoda, and Hakodadi. We therefore determined to locate at the latter port, where our whale ships have been appointed to rendezvous on the close of the present whaling season, and where they expect to receive from us in the fall, their supplies of provisions, chandlery, &c.

On our voyage thither, we touched at this port, March 15th, and on our arrival, found the crew of the late Russian Frigate Diana, who were wrecked on this island in Decr. last.

Our vessel was chartered to convey the Russians to one of their ports. We landed our cargo without opposition, and ourselves came on shore the 26th of March, have peaceably occupied one of the Temples assigned to us, until the 23d ult. since which time, a Correspondence has ensued between the Governor of Simoda, and ourselves, a copy of which, with original letters, you will please find enclosed.

Now Sir, in the absence of a U.S. Consul, or Commissioner, to whom we might present our grievances, we must necessarily claim your protection.

Relying on your consideration and interest in behalf of your countrymen—

We have the honor to be

Sir with great respect

Your most Obdt Servts—

(signed) Reed & Dougherty,

(signed) H. H. Doty, In behalf of the Americans.

On the twenty-first of the Third Month, 1855, three lesser officials of Shimoda (Gohoru Saburo, Murayama Takitsuro, and Nakagawa Tatsuki) requested the Americans to leave Shimoda as soon as possible after the return of their vessel, the *Caroline E. Foote*. She had been leased to the stranded Russians at Heda so that they might be evacuated to safety at Petropavlovsk. The Japanese document also warned against an attempt to secure permanent residence at Hakodaté.

One of the Americans, H. H. Doty, wrote on April 23rd to the governors of Shimoda, explaining the reason for the American vessel's absence and agreeing to depart soon after her return.

The partners W. C. Reed and T. T. Dougherty replied to the governor on May 7th with a declaration which concluded proudly:

As free American citizens, we cannot concede to you, or any other Government, not excepting our own, the right to determine for us, those things which our own interests must decide.

Mr. Doty was evidently encouraged to enter a similar protest on the next day.

From the Gyōkusenji, a temple in Shimoda's neighboring hamlet of Kakizaki, which Townsend Harris converted into the first American consulate in Nippon (August 28, 1856), Messrs. Edward A. Edgerton, William E. Bidleman, and Horace W. Peabody on May 10th wrote in these similar words:

. . . We have not during the period of about two months that we have lived and resided here asked to stay in this place, considering we were free here to do so, as in other countries, and not subjected to such restrictions as the Dutch and Chinese are at Nagasaki, who there stay and reside, and are not restricted and confined to staying on Shipboard.

We also as being Americans, free as in other countries, would with all due respect and in accordance with the firm, lasting and sincere friendship between the two nations, and with sincere, cordial amity protest against any Japanese being sent to follow us in our walks, or to spy what we do (which is not permitted in other countries!), or to prevent our going where we please at all times both by land and water, within the limits of the Treaty.

And also against any restriction, confinement or direction which is not in a manner clear and positive (as resolved by the Treaty of Kanagawa), expressed in and fixed by the Said Treaty, in neither which nor in the Regulations agreed to in the third month after making the said Treaty do we find any restriction or confinement as regards the time of our staying in this place or in Hakodadi, or any hours of the day or night specified, or any direction as to our departure being regulated by the Japanese authorities, to whom we wish to pay all proper respect! but that Americans being free here as in other countries, and in accordance with the firm lasting and sincere friendship between the two countries, and the sincere, cordial amity between their people[s], are not subjected to confinement in relation thereto. . . .

U.S. Ship Vincennes
Simoda,
[His Excellency The Governor of Simoda]   May 20th, 1855
Sir!

I have received from the American citizens, temporarily residing in Simoda, the correspondence which has taken place between your Excellency and them. I have not been instructed by my government in relation to them. I can therefore only express my own views of their case. The powers with which my government has clothed me, makes it necessary for me to do this.

It is very plain to me and I presume it will also be plain to your Excellency, that the treaty with the United States was a grave paper, involving important facts. By this treaty the government of Japan acknowledged that it was willing to draw into closer union the bonds of peace, which united them to the United States.

Treaties are agreements between nations. A treaty is law between equals and neither party can construe it against the consent of the other. Should there be a difference between the United States and your government, it must be settled by the Japanese sending a minister plenipotentiary to the United States, or the United States sending one to Japan. The meaning being there agreed upon by both parties, both will aid in carrying it out.

Article fourth of the treaty of Kanagawa is this: "Those shipwrecked persons and other citizens of the United States shall be free as in other countries and not subject to confinement, but shall be amenable to just laws."

Article fifth: "shipwrecked mariners and other citizens of the United States temporarily living at Simoda and Hakodadi shall not be subject to such restrictions and confinement as the Dutch and Chinese are at Nangasaki, but shall be free &c &c."[50]

The Treaty expressly mentions citizens of the United States temporarily living at Simoda and Hakodadi and provides for their safety and for their accommodation.

It remains to find out the meaning of "temporarily living."[51] It is the custom in America and Europe for the citizens of one country to travel freely into other lands. They carry passports, which are papers declaring who they are; these passports also request all magistrates, governors and governments before whom they may come, to give them aid and protection in their lawful acts.

When these people are apprehended for crimes or illegal deeds they write to their Consul or Ambassador who takes care that they are properly tried by legal tribunals. If guilty they are punished by the laws, and if innocent they are acquitted and free from all harm or illtreatment or restraint.

These people traveling for pleasure or for learning or for mercantile business reside temporarily, where they choose. They hire houses or build them or live at inns. Students from our country go to England or to France or to Germany and study as many years as they like; some study the laws, some study medicine, some surgery, some history, some literature. We have thus a knowledge of all countries of all laws, of all literature, of all science. Some go abroad to study mechanic arts, some to study science, some to study warfare, some to study the arts of peace. All these men having resided tempo-

[50] Cf., Hunter Miller (ed.), *Treaties and Other International Acts* . . . , VI, p. 441.
[51] Article Two of the Shimoda Convention of June 17, 1857, provided that Americans might reside permanently at Shimoda and Hakodaté (*ibid.*, VII, p. 596); and the Treaty of Yedo, July 29, 1858, extended the privilege in five additional ports when they should be opened (*ibid.*, pp. 950-951).

rarily abroad bring to their country valuable information. In the same manner we impart our knowledge as freely as we seek it. Foreign citizens may have a temporary residence in our country as long as they please; So our citizens live temporarily in other countries as long as they please.

We have laws, by which foreign citizens may become naturalized. It offers them advantages, should they wish to remain in our country; then after naturalization they are no longer temporary residents and cannot claim the interposition of their former government. They become Americans by naturalization.

Our citizens temporarily living in Mexico and carrying on trade there or living quietly for their pleasure, were unjustly treated; for a long time we endeavoured to obtain, what the treaty allowed. The Mexican government refused to listen to our remonstrances, many cases occurred. At last after fruitless attempts to obtain justice, we made war, took all their fortresses, which opposed us, took their capital, the city of Mexico and overran their country. The Mexicans supposed, we would suffer them to illtreat our temporary citizens and thought, because we were a very peaceable people, that we would not punish them. Having overcome them we made peace. The temporary residence mentioned in the treaty of Kanagawa had reference I think on the part of the Government of the United States to "temporary residence" in Hakodadi and Simoda, such as exists elsewhere, with liberty to move within certain limits, specified and with the right, to buy through the government what they needed and amenable only to just laws; but if the Government of Japan does not so understand it, their understanding is a fair subject of deliberation and I am sure that from the high opinion which my government has of the justice and friendship and kindness of His Imperial Majesty the Emperor of Japan, his interpretation will receive the President's most earnest attention.

Now it seems that the American gentlemen here have come to Japan upon a fair interpretation of the treaty, as understood in the United States, and they have not willfully done any wrong. I think that they have done what the treaty meant to allow them to do. The Japanese government has a perfect right to think differently. But there are two parties to the treaty. Two equal governments have made the law. When the governments agree as to the interpretation, it will then be plain what should be done. But now the United States cannot carry them away, until the Japanese government consents and the Japanese cannot send them away until it is agreed what the treaty means by "temporary residence." Because both governments are concerned, the matter is too high for either government alone. The Americans alone cannot interpret the treaty, neither can the Japanese alone. The Japanese government can remonstrate with the American government. By remonstrance I mean that His Imperial Majesty the Emperor of Japan may write to the President of the United States, or the Japanese highest Officer for Foreign Affairs can write to the American Secretary of State, who is our highest Officer for Foreign Affairs, Or His Excellency the Governor of Simoda can write to the American Secretary of State for Foreign Affairs and say he writes by order of his government.

Where an Officer has an opportunity of learning the opinion of his government he cannot write his own views, or if he does it will not be regarded. But an Officer like myself, who is so far away from his country, must write his own opinion, because he cannot receive orders upon the sudden things, which happen. I am required by my government to do this. In suffering these Americans to reside temporarily in Simoda or in Hakodadi, it is plain that the Japanese government cannot receive any harm. The people are too few and if the Japanese government remonstrates, then it cannot be brought into a precedent, because the Japanese government says that it does not understand the treaty as we understand it and they wish to have the meaning settled. After knowing the meaning then can the Japanese send them away, if it is so decided.

When a treaty gives a thing, it gives every thing which is

necessary to the enjoyment of the thing given. If a person may live in a place it is plain, he must have a right to sleep and to eat; he must have a house and provisions and fuel. Thus a permission to live at Simoda and Hakodadi must give all the means of living. If a permission has any meaning, it intends protections and permission to reside in houses and to buy food.

I think the wise way would be for the Governors of Simoda and Hakodadi to be patient and to avoid rash deeds. The American government is just and peaceable and honorable, as well as strong. Let them remonstrate in the name of their government, as I now remonstrate in the name of my government. I will send their paper to my government and the matter will be settled by the Emperor of Japan and the President of the United States. The Governors will avoid breaking the treaty before it is understood and friendship will grow stronger and stronger.

If American vessels go to Simoda and Hakodadi, it is plain, that they must have the things necessary for them, such as the Japanese do not use and cannot supply: Chain Cables and iron anchors, such as our large ships employ, are not made in Japan and therefore the Japanese cannot supply them. Cordage and salt provisions and bread and tar with many other things are necessary to American vessels. Let these Americans live quietly here or go to Hakodadi, let them do every thing which Americans think is in the treaty. Remonstrate with the American government and it will be time enough to get angry and do things by force, after the remonstrance fails to receive attention. That the Americans thought they were right is proved by their bringing their wives and children. They would not have brought them, had they contemplated breaking the laws.

I am required by the government of the United States to write to them every thing which I do, to send copies of every writing which I may receive, and to report all my acts. By this time I think the President of the United States knows of my letter to the Honorable Secretary of State for Foreign Affairs Empire of Japan, for I sent it [home] from Hong Kong, before I came to Simoda. This letter which I now write is too important to be neglected. I shall send a copy of it from Hakodadi and also a copy of the correspondence which the American gentlemen temporarily residing in Japan had the honor of holding with your Excellency.

My position and my necessity of reporting all I do makes me careful in my acts and scrupulous in what I write. What I have said is worthy of your Excellency's serious attention. I beg Your Excellency to receive the assurances of my highest respect and to believe me

Sincerely Your Friend,

Signed, JOHN RODGERS,
Commanding U.S. Surveying Expedition
to the North Pacific Ocean &c &c.

His Excellency
The Governor of Simoda

U.S. Ship Vincennes
Hakodadi

[His Excellency The Governor of Hakodaté]   June 15th, 1855
Sir!

Several American[s] have come from the United States to "reside temporarily" in Hakodadi under the stipulations of the treaty made in regard to them.

I have the honor to request Your Excellency to permit them to "live temporarily" in the city under your governance.

I have the honor to be

Your Excellency's
Sincere Friend,

(Signed) JOHN RODGERS,
Commanding U.S. Surveying Expedition
to China Seas, & Pacific Ocean

His Excellency
The Governor
of Hakodadi.

On the same day came the reply from Governor Takenouchi, Shimotsuke-no-kami, which was translated by the Americans from the Dutch.

To His Excellency
the Commodore of the American
Ship of war Vincennes.

About the residence of the American[s] and women here in Hakodaté and about the letter written by Your Excellency to the Governor of Simoda I have written to day to the Japanese Government. Since the said Governor has probably already reported about the residence of these people, I require the decision of the Government. I have said that until the decision arrives I cannot grant a residence to others than shipwrecked people. Your Excellency states that a written answer is necessary to be sent to the United States, and that in consequence a fleet of war would arrive. The reasons for this I do not comprehend. Said Governor has not permitted the residents of the Americans in Simoda, but on account of the unfortunate Russians in Simoda the Americans from the Schooner were taken on shore. When the Governor asked the Russians for the reason of it, the Russians said that misfortune and season (possibly earthquake of the season) had forced them to do so; they wished in case any other nation should urge this as a precedent, before the permission was obtained, that the Governor should state, the Russians had done wrong. Even Your Officer (Consul) shall not reside in Simoda before eighteen months, as the treaty stipulates there is no right in my opinion to reside without permission in Hakodaté. Respecting the manner of your Government and the necessity for ships, it is hereby communicated to your Excellency, that I have promptly written the Government and that I cannot permit a free residence before I receive the decision of the Government as to whet[h]er your interpretation of the residence in Hakodaté shall take place. I cannot comprehend that a fleet of war shall arrive from the United States because I uphold the law, while both empires are very friendly; and finally it is my wish, that it may be shown, in case the wrong should be on our side.

(signed) Takenowoetsy Simotske-no-kami
[Takenouchi Shimotsuke-no-kami]
Governor of Hakodaté

Ansei 9th, 2nd day
of 5th month [June 15, 1855].

Almost immediately after seconding the application of his countrymen, Commander Rodgers asked on their behalf for a six-month permit of residence. Governor Takenouchi's answer, which follows, was delivered by his so-called "first officer" during a conference with Rodgers on June 17th.

To
His Excellency
the Commodore of the
American Ship of war Vincennes

Your Excellency has demanded, that certain Americans may reside "temporarily" in the town subject to Japanese law according to Article 5 of the treaty. I understand by the word "temporarily" five or seven days to the utmost a few months. Shipwrecked people and such others as are compelled by circumstances to remain, may live temporarily. It is known, that at your request three Americans were permitted to stay until the arrival of the Schooner.

Since the Americans who now wish to stay in town, have come with their wives and children, they purport to stay not temporarily, but longer. Thus according to the treaty, it is not possible for them to stay.

(Signed) Takenowoetsy Simotske-no-kami
[Takenouchi Shimotsuke-no-kami]
Governor of Hakodaté

Ansei 9th,
4th day of 5th Month
[June 17, 1855]

The first Officer of Hakodadi, Tsikaraise Katsnoska [Chikaraise Katsunosuke] came on board the U.S. Ship Vincennes, June 17th, 1855, and delivered from the Governor of Hakodadi, an answer in Dutch, and Japanese, to the letter from John Rodgers, Commanding U.S. Surveying Expedition, to the North Pacific Ocean, and China Seas, requesting permission for certain American citizens to live on shore, in Hakodadi, under the treaty of Kanagawa.

The letters relating there to, are appended. In the conversation which ensued, the first Officer stated through the Japanese interpreter, Namoera Gohatsjra [Namura Gōhachirō], that the manners of Europeans were different from those of the Japanese. That the Japanese officers who lived temporarily in other cities than the capital, had to leave their wives, and children. That therefore these Americans who came to Hakodadi could not live on shore because they brought their families, which argued not a temporary residence, but a permanent one.

It was explained by me that the laws of different countries varied, and that no nation could interpret a treaty by its own municiple law, otherwise treaties would mean differently in two countries, that any nation had only in such a case to alter its law, to evade a treaty. That therefore treaties were interpreted by a code, called the law of nations.

It was further answered on my part, that women, and children, were citizens in America, and Europe, that as such, we claimed the treaty in their favor. It was further explained that the highest personage in Great Britain, was a woman. By Japanese laws, any treaty in favor of British subjects, would exclude their Sovereign, and her family from its benefits.

They answered, that Japanese women, and children, were also citizens of Japan. But Americans with their women, and children, could not live in Hakodadi. "Temporarily," was explained by me to mean an indefinite time, to be arranged between the two governments. That in excluding the American citizens from a temporary residence, the Governor was taking the responsibility of acting upon the Japanese interpretation. I explained that to act his opinion was different from expressing it. I thought the Americans had the right to live on shore. Were I to fire upon them for refusal, I would then act upon my opinion.

It was replied that the Governor could not permit the Americans to live on shore.

I asked whether the Governor would suffer the Americans to reside on shore until the interpretation of "temporarily living" arrived from Jedo. The first Officer said that they could walk in, and about the town as they pleased, but not sleep a single night on shore.

It was explained that a number of Whaling vessels, about 40, had made a contract with Messrs. Reed, and Dougherty, to be supplied here, with such things as the Japanese do not use, such as large anchors, chains, hemp cordage, &c., and that it would be a great disappointment to them.

It was answered that the Japanese Governor was very sorry, but that he could not give permission for the Americans to live on shore. That he would write to Jedo. But that he did not know what the answer would be.

I explained that the American government was an equal party to the treaty, and claimed a joint voice in its interpretation. I explained that should the American government support my views of the meaning, I presumed it would be aggrieved by the sole action of the government of Japan.

It was answered by the first Officer, that the Governor was very sorry, and that the Americans had his good wishes, but that he could not permit them to live on shore.

I asked whether the gentlemen could stay without their families, the answer was that they could not, for a longer time than the Governors definition of "temporary," that is 5, or 7, days, at the utmost a few months, should I define it so.

They wished me to define "temporary" to mean some definite period, after which the Americans should go away.

I answered that I had written a letter to explain my idea of what "temporary" means, but that I could not use in my request in regard to these Americans, an expression different from the one which the President, and Emperor, had employed. They had in their wisdom used the word "temporary." Therefore, I asked that the Americans might live "temporarily" on shore, until the meaning was settled.

The first Officer answered that the Governor gave the Americans his good wishes, that he was sorry he could not permit them to come on shore. He had no power to do so.

When I further asked whether the Americans would be permitted to go on shore, and to remain quietly without express permission, until an answer from Jedo arrived, the answer was that the Governor would not suffer it. That the Governor gave us his good wishes, permission he could not give.

(Signed) JOHN RODGERS
Commanding U.S. Surveying Expedition
to China Seas, and Pacific Ocean.

Commander Rodgers relayed to the Navy Department the Japanese version of the same conference. It had been translated first into Dutch and then into English. The American officer claimed that two errors were made in the Japanese account.

On the day following the interview (June 18th), Messrs. Edgerton, Peabody, and Bidleman wrote to the Governor requesting a house at Hakodaté for temporary residence. Apparently this accompanied still another communication from Rodgers, in which he thus explained his obligation to intervene in such matters:

... The same interest which you see exhibited in Japan, is shown every where else, whether in Empires, or amongst Canibals, whether in Europe, or Asia, or Africa, or the most distant Islands of the uttermost seas. Every where is the Flag their shield, and bond of protection to the high Officers at home. This is my excuse for again troubling your Excellency.

The gist of the conversation between Commander Rodgers and the "first officer" was transmitted two days after the meeting (on June 19th) to Messrs. W. C. Reed (and family), T. T. Dougherty, E. A. Edgerton, H. W. Peabody, and W. E. Bidleman; it prompted the following reply:

Hakodadi
[Commander John Rodgers]   June 19th, 1855
Sir!
Having placed in your possession the correspondence had between ourselves, and the Japanese authorities at Samoda, and also informed you of our intention to remove from that place soon and establish ourselves at Hakodadi, we placed ourselves under your protection and have relied upon your superior judgement and tact in gaining a residence for us here.

In the correspondence received this day from you upon this subject, we learned that on no condition whatever are we to be permitted to reside on shore, and we must therefore abide your better judgement, and leave without making an effort within ourselves so to do, or without by actually trying to go on shore, and thereby tempting the Japanese to use violence to our family, and ourselves.

Your statement, corroborated by Capt. Stevens, cannot fail to convince our Government of the proper means used to obtain a residence here, under the Fourth (4th), and Fifth (5th), article[s] of the Treaty of Kanagawa, and of their utter refusal to carry out the provisions of said articles.

Now therefore having placed ourselves under your direction, and as American citizens relying upon our Flags protection, we submit to your decision without making further personal efforts to land.

But while we submit to this indignity, this most humiliating, and degrading thwart of the Japanese government, this Bar to our commercial transactions, to carry out which we have invested all our resources, have perilled the lives of our family, and suffered many inconveniences, and failing, may incur damages for far beyond our means to liquidate.

Therefore we do solemnly protest against the action of the Japanese government, and their right to refuse us a quiet temporary residence on their shores, and of embarrassing our transactions, and will hold our Government responsible for all damages arising from this refusal, and claim this to be to all intents, and purposes, our protest against the Japanese Government, reserving to ourselves, the right of Extending this Protest, at any future time, and place.

We have the honor to be

Sir,

With great respect,

Your Obdt Servt[s]

(Signed) REED & DOUGHERTY

(Signed) HORACE W. PEABODY

John Rodgers
Commanding U.S. Exploring Expedition
to the North Pacific Ocean &c, &c, &c, &c.

A copy of the above protest was forwarded by Commander Rodgers on June 25th to "His Excellency the Governor of Hakodadi." Reed and Dougherty also made a formal deposition, stating their complaints in the presence of Rodgers on the same day. In the letter which follows, Rodgers tried to reassure his countrymen:

U.S. Ship Vincennes
Hakodadi
June 25th, 1855

[The American Citizens at Hakodaté]
Gentlemen!

I am afraid that my intervention on behalf of the American citizens who came here to reside temporarily under the treaty of Kanagawa may at first sight appear luke warm.

The Governor of this place and Simoda are mere agents,

and do not, I am sure, act upon their own responsibility. To have affected my wishes I should have been obliged to go to Jedo and to appeal to the fears of the Emperor.

It was not admissable for any mere casual man-of-war to expound without instructions and interpretation of a formal treaty at the çannon's mouth. The question which you have raised is one affecting vitally the policy of two nations. I had no instructions from the Government.

I think it would be easy to take Hakodadi with the forces at my command, but they were not confided for such a purpose, except to redress personal illtreatment of my countrymen.

I have told the Government of the city that I should send armed men on shore, if certain rudenesses, which were personal wrongs, were persisted in; but the interpretation of the treaty belongs to the Governments. This is a public wrong, not merely a private one.

I think you have been illtreated, and that through you and to your loss has been shown, that valuable results are not to be expected from the treaty. Wood, water and shelter for ships is all we may hope from the Japanese reading of it.

I am American enough to think that in referring your case to the Government of the United States I confide you to safe hands.

I have the honor to be,

Gentlemen

your obedient servant,

(Signed) JOHN RODGERS

To the American citizens
    in Hakodadi
               Comdg. U.S. Surveying Expedition
                   to the North Pacific Ocean.

[Secretary Dobbin]

Sir!

I have to enclose a very disagreeable correspondence in regard to G. B. Babi, and Francis Vidan.

These people were passengers in the American Brig "Leveret." They came to settle in Japan under the treaty. They came from Honolulu, they are evidently foreigners, and have not a show of evidence that they have ever been naturalized.

I inferred from their bringing no stores but liquors, that they entended to retail it in Japan, in other words, to set up a grog shop for the benefit of any casual sailors who might wander on shore.

They were refused permission to reside on shore by the Japanese. Having landed, they were brought off to the John Hancock.

Capt. Stevens very properly refused to receive them. They were taken to the Leveret, and left on board.

The Capt. of the Leveret asked for me to interfere. Messrs. Babi, and Vidan said that they had no wish to remain in Japan; but only desired to live on shore for a few days, until an opportunity arose for getting either to Europe, or China, or America.

They earnestly requested me at several interviews to obtain this boon for them.

The Captain declared that his voyage to the Ockholsk was ruined with them on board, that he could not take them, that his cabin was already so crowded that his mates were excluded from their proper accommodations.

These gentlemen, Messrs. Babi and Vidan, said that to get away, they would live any where, and with any accommodation, in any vessel which came here.

As a matter of humanity I consented to write to the Japanese Governor in their favor, stating that they were to live only a few days on shore. The letter is appended.

After the arrival of the "Foote," they refused to abide by the word, which at their request I had pledged to the Japanese Government. They declared they would stay.

They have constantly made the sailors drunk by selling them liquor.

My position was difficult. It was not proper for me to allow the faith of an Officer to be questioned by the Japanese, who had pledged himself for them [Babi and Vidan] upon their own repeated and urgent solicitations.

It was not proper for me to declare that they were not Americans, both because I by my action deceived the Japanese or acquiesced in their deception as to their nationality; as well as because I could not tell how inhumanly they might be treated.

It was not proper for me to leave these foreign grog shop keepers to stay on shore as Americans upon a residence obtained by fraud and falsehood, as the first representatives of American citizens.

It was not proper to leave them under our flag to debauch our seamen, and complicate our difficulties.

At the solicitation of the Japanese Government I thought myself obliged to inform them that I should use force to take them to the C. E. Foote, unless they would save me the pain of so acting.

I have the honor to be

Very Respectfully
Your Obdt. Servt.

JOHN RODGERS
Comdg. U.S. Surveying Expedition
to North Pacific Ocean &c.

Honorable James C. Dobbin
Secretary of the Navy
Washington, D.C.

To the Commander of the American Steamship
[Translation from the Dutch]
Sir:

I have promptly received your two letters and perceive from their contents that you think it improper that two American citizens have been brought by a Japanese boat to your ship. The said citizens were brought off for the following reasons.

Lately these citizens came on shore and demanded to stay over night. So it was reported to one of our officers. You know that except shipwrecked people nobody is allowed to stay over night. In the meantime these citizens stated that since their boat had gone away, they wished to be sent on board of the American steamer by a Japanese boat. So they were brought to your ship in accordance with their own will.

(signed) TAKENOWOETSJ [Takenouchi]
SIMODSKENOKAMI [Shimotsuke-no-kami]
Hakodadi
Ansei 9th year 23rd of the
fourth month [June 7, 1855]

U.S. Ship Vincennes
Hakodadi
June 11th, 1855

[The Governor of Hakodaté]
Sir!

Two passengers in the American Brig "Leveret," G. B. Babi, and Francis Vidan, find that from circumstances, it is impossible for them to continue on board the vessel in which they came here.

They wish to live on shore, until an opportunity offers for them to go to Europe, China, or America.

Having no wish to stay, they will eagerly embrace the first suitable opportunity for leaving.

They will not transgress any law of good conduct. But in case they should do so, the Japanese have authority to confine

[122]

them in their houses until it becomes possible to send them away.

With assurances of the highest respect, I have the honor to be—Your Excellenceys

Sincere friend,

JOHN RODGERS
Commanding U.S. Surveying Expedition
to the North Pacific Ocean &c &c.

To His Excellency
The Governor of Hakodadi

U.S. Ship Vincennes
Hakodadi
June 12th, 1855

[The Governor of Hakodaté]

Sir!

The American Schooner, Caroline Foote, is expected here every day. Should she be able to take the passengers landed from the American Brig "Leveret," and they be able to secure a passage in her, it is their wish to do so.

I have the honor to be Your Excellencys

Sincere friend,

(signed) JOHN RODGERS

Commanding U.S. Surveying Expedition
to the North Pacific Ocean &c.

To His Excellency
The Governor of Hakodadi

U.S. Ship Vincennes
Hakodadi
June 24th, 1855

[The Governor of Hakodaté]

Sir!

The suitable opportunity to which I had reference in my letter to Your Excellency of the 11th. inst. for the embarkation of G. B. Babie and Francis Vidan has arrived.

[123]

I have no wish that they should remain longer. I have the
honor to be

Your Excellency's

Sincere Friend,

(signed) JOHN RODGERS

To
His Excellency
the Governor
of Hakodadi

Commdg. U.S. Surveying Expd.
to the North Pacific Ocean.

U.S. Ship Vincennes
Hakodadi
June 24th, 1855

[Messrs. Vidan and Babi]
Gentlemen,

The Japanese have informed me that you now refuse positively to embark for San Francisco in the Schooner C. E.
Foote.

I do not consider that you have obtained a fair footing in
Japan. It was upon my representation of your being willing to
go away in the first vessel to Europe, America, or China.

I hope therefore, that you will not consider it necessary to
drive me to extreme measures.

Very respectfully
Your obedient servant,

(signed) JOHN RODGERS

To Mrsrs. Vidal [*sic*] and Babi
Hakodadi

Commdg. Surv. Expn.

U.S. Ship Vincennes
Hakodadi
June 24th, 1855

[Messrs. Babi and Vidan]
Gentlemen:

You doubtless recollect the terms upon which I consented
to intercede with the Japanese Government for permission for

you to reside on shore. You stated that you wished to leave [at] the first opportunity.

After repeated solicitation I wrote to the Japanese Government and obtained permission for you to live on shore; but as I had no cause to consider you citizens of the United States and as you were without even a shadow of proof of naturalization, I expressly stated, that I considered your residence on shore as a personal favor from the Governor and not as a right, demanded from the Government of Japan.

At your urgent solicitation I pledged my word for you, that you would go away by the first oportunity. Mr. Babie also said that you had plenty of money.

You have come on shore at my intercession, but you refuse to carry out the promise, which at your own solicitation I had plighted for you and you have been selling liquor to the crew and you have caused a great deal of trouble.

Under all these circumstances of your stay being protracted in fraud, of your living under the American flag, to whose protection you have no right, and of your occupation of selling grog not being the one which I would see first introduced into Japan under the auspices of the Government of the United States, I am compelled to order you to repair on board the Foote for passage to California.

I am your
Obdt. Servt,
(signed) JOHN RODGERS
Lt. Commdg. Surv. Expdn.

Mesrs: Babi & Vidal [*sic*]

U.S. Ship Vincennes
Hakodadi
June 23rd, 1855

[Secretary Dobbin]
Sir!

I have the honor of informing you that I deem our hydrographic operations this summer have been fortunate.

We have corrected many positions. We have executed a running survey of both sides of the Empire of Japan to this place.

The launch, in charge of Lt. Brooke, has made a most successful surveying voyage of 450 miles from Simoda to Hakodadi.

It follows of course that our materials accumulate faster than we can chart them, and I am compelled to delay the presentation of finished work.

The large Island of Ousima, has three excellent harbors, one is a sound seperating Ousima from Katona-Sima, which the Cooper and Vincennes entered from different sides, on the same day at about the same hour. It runs quite through, and is filled with land locked harbors where the navies of the world might ride out hurricanes. Another harbor is at the NW end of Ousima; it is large, well marked,'deep, easily entered, and protected from all winds. Another near the SW end of the Island was examined by the Hancock and found to be very fine.

In Porpoise Sound, which was so-called after our lost vessel, we asked for water, and the authorities sent off about 5 gallons. We asked for provisions, and they gave a bunch of turnips. We gravely demanded the price of our refreshments for the crew. They were gratuitous. Wood and water are abundant.

The people are jealous, and timid, and very poor. They regret doubtless, that the world has found them.

The Japanese have, it is said, ceded the Kurile Islands to Russia by their late treaty. I believe they are compensating themselves to the southward.[52]

[52] By the treaty concluded at Shimoda at the instance of Admiral E. V. Putiatin, February 7, 1855, the Russians were to be recognized in possession of those Kurile Islands north of the island of Urup, while the Japanese retained title to the island of Iturup and those lying between it and Ezo.

Not until 1875 did the Tsarist government trade its claims in the Kuriles (Chishima) for uncontested title to all of Sakhalin Island. As a result of the Russo-Japanese War, Japan (by the Treaty of Portsmouth) received that part of Sakhalin south of 50° North Latitude; this region was named Karafutō. Karafutō was reoccupied by Soviet Russian troops in August 1945 and is being

We found a Japanese town on Ousima. In Kikay the authorities wear swords, and dress their hair as Japanese. They state that Kikay is a Loo-Chooan Island. While the Loo-Chooans denied authority over the Island of Ousima, the people of Ousima said they belonged to Loo-Choo. I think it probable from what I have seen that the Japanese are gradually absorbing the more peaceable and unresisting islands to the southward of their Empire. This opinion is strengthened by the Missionaries in Loo-Choo, who say that the allegiance of this Kingdom is really paid to Japan, while the Loo-Chooans themselves declare that they owe it to China. I believe that this is peaceable absorbtion by a more vigorous race, and that while the law of fealty to China remains, its essence is transferred to Japan.[53]

The Japanese may thus follow a very wide and general law, by giving way to their more powerful neighbours on the North, and encroaching on their weaker ones to the South. Only thus can I account for the contradictory statements which are given of the political sovereignty of the Islands to the Sd. of Japan.

I sent the Japanese Secretary of State for Foreign Affairs, the letter in relation to surveying in Japanese waters, which is appended.[54]

I became uneasy at not receiving an answer. Delay would be fatal. I determined to appear to wait, and in the mean

retained by the Soviet Union. The Soviet Union, according to the Yalta Agreement, has also occupied the Kurile Islands.

[53] Since the fourteenth century, rulers of the Liu Ch'iu Islands had paid intermittent tribute to the Ming and later the Ch'ing emperors of China. However, in 1609, the daimyō (feudal lord) of the fief of Satsuma had sent his samurai, who conquered the islands. Thereafter the Liu Ch'iuan rulers had two masters, although it was quite apparent to officers who visited along with Perry and Rodgers that Liu Ch'iuan policies were being shaped more by Japanese than by Chinese pressure. Samurai, probably from Satsuma, were noticed by the Americans at Naha.

Not until 1876 was Japan's claim to the Liu Ch'ius legally recognized by the Manchu-Chinese government. In 1862 the Japanese government asserted its claims to the Bonin (Ōgasawara) group.

[54] See Rodgers' communication to the "Honourable Secretary of State of the Empire of Japan," written at Hongkong, February 7, 1855; supra, pp. 49-52.

while seize the few points our limited time would allow us to enjoy.

The Governor was lead in an interview, to say we had better go away, and return for our answer. I said in that case we should do so, but that I would send a boat to Hakodadi to look at the rocks and dangers in shore of us.

Having no time for minute survey in thus running along the coast, and sending a boat to examine the bays, and harbors, I was securing all that the fullest permission would allow us to use. We have thus escaped both the difficulties which menaced us, in case they refused to let us examine their waters, and the procrastination of Japanese diplomacy.

My efforts in behalf of the Americans who had come here to reside, have not been so fortunate.

I hope it will be considered that the necessity for my intervention arose from the state of the case, and was thrust upon me by circumstances of which I was ignorant until my arrival in Simoda, and over which I had no control. I have not sought noteriety by complicating our foreign relations. I have simply done what I thought my duty as well as I could. My action has had no effect other than to point out that the Japanese do not understand their treaty as we understand it, and that they repudiate, or nullify, the meaning which I believe is attached to it in the United States.

It could scarcely be otherwise, and the result will not surprise any one who has read books on Japan.

I am aware of how serious a matter it is for a nation to nullify a foreign treaty, and I have been very cautious I hope, in my judgement and in my acts.

We start to morrow for Petropaulaski, thence to the Arctic Sea, thence to San Francisco, where I hope to arrive in October.

I believe that all the Officers and men of all the vessels are full of zeal and good will. The fewness of Officers is a great draw back, but I have every confidence that should you hear incidentally of us, it will be favorably.

I propose from San Francisco to survey the Southern route to Shanghai, through the trades in the three belts.

To Shanghai, because interesting points lie on the route, and because opinion points to that as the Chinese Emporium of American Commerce.

From Shanghai to Hong Kong, to fill up with provisions, thence to Manilla, thence through the Sooloo Sea, and Caroline Islands, to Valparaiso. Thence to Rio Janeiro, thence home.[55]

This will fill up our cruise I hope with usefulness. It will devote our labors to the Ocean upon which we have important possessions, and are the only powerful race; to the Ocean in which we of all the world have the deepest interest.

I hope you will forward to me authority to sell the Hancock in China, or in Valparaiso, at my discretion, or to send her to San Francisco to discharge her crew.

Her work to Valparaiso would be most valuable, so also will be the Coopers be.

The two Gallant officers of this small vessel wish to have the honor of carrying her home; of performing the circumnavigation of the globe in the smallest vessel upon record.

Should the Cooper reach Valparaiso safely, the Burthen of her risk will have been borne, and the rest will have no difficulty.

I append interesting reports of the Commanding Officers.[56]

I have the honor to be

Very Respectfully
Your obdt servt,

JOHN RODGERS
Commanding U.S. Surveying Expedition
to the North Pacific Ocean

Honorable James C. Dobbin
Secretary of the Navy
Washington, D.C.

[55] As explained in the introduction, this program had to be curtailed, but apparently plans were not modified until after the squadron reassembled at San Francisco.
[56] Because of the timing of events which they describe, the reports from these

U.S. Ship Vincennes
Hakodadi
[Lieutenant H. K. Stevens]   June 25th, 1855
Sir!

You will complete your reconnaissance of the Straits of Sangar [Tsūgarū], and then pass on the west side of this island [Ezo, Yezo, or Hokkaidō] through the Straits of La Perouse into the Sea of Ochotsk. You will probably find coal on the East side, in Lat. 60. 17. and about 161, 30, E Long, and on the west side, in 60. 28. Lat, and 156.28. E Long—

In the Gulf of Tartary, on the Island of Saghalien, coal may also be found. Its locality can doubtless be ascertained from the Russians.

In consequence of the active state of war existing in the vicinity of the Amour, it will not be prudent to venture there immediately.[57] The English would naturally have the fear that you might convey valuable information to the Russians, and the Russians, lest you should betray something which they wished to keep secret. There are other reasons, the fogs are now very dense. In the Northern part you have a clear sea, and in case of a gale, by simply putting the vessels head off shore, you will be safe. Near the Amour, the Sea is encumbered with sand banks, but when you arrive there the fogs will have dispersed.

From the Ochotsk I wish you if possible to penetrate to the Sd. into the Gulf of Tartary as far as Castries. Beyond this I do not care particularly for your examination, since that Gulf has been laid down by able men. I therefore leave it to yourself to come entirely through it or return, and pass the Amour—

The objects to be sought are so well known to you, and my

officers have been shifted forward in the present volume. The report of Lieutenant H. K. Stevens will be found in *supra*, pp. 67-71; that of Acting Lieutenant William Gibson, on pages 71-87; and that of Acting Lieutenant John M. Brooke, on pages 87-98.

[57] The Crimean War also affected international relations in the Pacific area.

views have been so fully expressed that more is unnecessary. I hope every thing from your judgment, tact, and skill. Many difficulties may arise which I have not foreseen. Your own discretion must guide you in such Cases.

Make your way in about 50 North, to Long. 150, west, thence to San Francisco in October.

My last instructions pointed out details I have omitted here—

Very Respectfully,
Your obdt. Servt.

(signed) JOHN RODGERS
Comdg. U.S. Surveying Expedition
to North Pacific Ocean &c

To
Lieut. Comdg. H. K. Stevens
U.S. Steamer John Hancock

U.S. Ship Vincennes
Hakodadi
[Acting Lieutenant William Gibson]   June 25th, 1855

Sir!

I find no cause to modify the instructions which I gave you in Hong Kong relative to your present course.

You will proceed from this place to Petropaulaski, where we shall meet, you to take up the survey of the Aleutian islands, and search for the crew of the American Whaler Monongahela, We to penetrate into the Arctic Ocean.

We shall meet I hope in San Francisco early in October next.

Lutke says "on dit qu'il y a dans l'ile d'Akoun des couches de charbon de terre"—

The fact of coal beds there, or elsewhere in the group, is vital and demands your most earnest attention.

I wish you to call during the season at Sitka, to obtain all such hydrographic information as you can. The attack of the

English, as far as your success in this object is concerned, is much to be deplored by us, and will probably prevent any great hydrographic acquisitions.

The English if in possession of the hydrographic office there, may feel inclined to be generous in giving Russian Charts.

Go up inside of the Kurile Islands, if you get a chance of running through them. But fogs might possibly delay you more than is desirable at the present time. We have been retarded so much that now the main objects must be principally looked to, and we have to pass rapidly through inviting fields until we arrive at the ground allotted to us.

I thank you for your important contributions to the objects for which we were sent from home.

Your usefulness has been in an inverse ratio to the size of your vessel. May it continue so.

Wishing you, your Shipmates, and your gallant bark every success.

I remain

Respectfully
Your Obdt. Servt,

(signed) JOHN RODGERS
Comdg. U.S. Surveying Expedition
to North Pacific Ocean, &c.

To Actg. Lieut. Comdg.
    William Gibson
    U.S. Schooner Fenimore Cooper

Before leaving Hakodaté Commander Rodgers wrote to "His Excellency General Murawieff [Muraviev], Governor General of Siberia," thanking him for having detailed two officers to assist the Americans in the exploration of northern waters. Unfortunately, said Rodgers, activities in the China Seas had detained the squadron, making it impossible to avail itself of the offered services.

As a reciprocal gesture, Rodgers forwarded to Muraviev (the

Count of the Amur) a set of charts made by the coastal survey of the United States together with a small book on Chinese costumes printed on rice paper.

Muraviev's cordial response from Port Ayan on the Siberian coast reached the expedition some time after its arrival at San Francisco.

P. Ayan, the 20th October a   1855.
                   1st November

[Mr. John Rodgers]

My dear Sir!

Acknowledging the receipt of Your letter, dated Petropaulofsky the 11/23 of July, I avail my self of this opportunity to thank you for the friendly feelings You have therein expressed toward me.

I regret much that the letters I addressed to Commodore Perry could not reach him last year, and it is only now in answering You, that I have the opportunity to repair this unluck.

You wisch to receive the Charts which I sent with my Aide-de-Camps last year to Ochotsk and Ayan in order to be delivered there to Com. Perry, but they were in the autumn returned to Tezkoutsk, and consequently are not now at hand. I am not at this moment able to fulfill Your desire for the rest; they were intended only to give You an idea of the Coastline of Siberia and can I presume be of no use to You since you have completed the survey of the Ochotsk Sea. As for the chart of the entrance of Amoor river, it is yet so incorrect that I do not think it deserves to get a place in your valuable work, and consequently I do not dare to lay it before you.

Allow me Sir to express my cordial thanks for the charts, the Chineese curiosities, and the excellent rifel, You was so kind to hand over to my Aide-de-Camp Mr[.] Martinoff in Petropawlofsky; he did not yet send them to me in fear that they might fall in the hands of our enemy.

Sir besure that I perfectly understand how to value these marks of your friendschip towards me.

I hope, Sir, that You will make me the honor of accepting

[a] knife from the workschop of a *Russian Master* Sazikoff, whose works got the price-medal at the Universal Exhibition in London.

It would be superfluous for me to assure you of the friendly relations existing between the Government of Russia and that of the United States; they are as well known to you as they are to me, and it remains only for me to repeat once more my warmest thanks for Your Kind letter and assure you of the high consideration with which I have the honor to be,

Sir,

Your obedient servant,

(signed) NICOLAS MAURAVIEFF

to Mr. John Rodgers
   Lt. Com. U.S. Surv.
   Exped. to China seas
   and Pacific Ocean.

U.S. Ship Vincennes
San Francisco California
December 11th, 1855

[Nicolas Muraviev]

Your Excellency,

I have the honor to thank you for the magnificent hunting knife you were so kind as to send me, and which I have had the happiness of receiving.

As a work of art it is very beautiful. Made in Russia, it would do honor to the studios of Italy.

As a testimony of your regard, I shall always cherish it, and as a memento of the friendly feeling, which animates our governments, I hold it invaluable.

Our work in the Ochotsk was not so extensive as our Whaling vessels could wish it had been.

I have been lead to believe that a chart of Amour will have little practical value since the obstructions to navigation continually shift their place. In such cases, pilots, are the only means which vessels have of ascertaining the channel.

In the Arctic Ocean we were enabled to get within ten

miles of the position which Baron Wrangel assigns to the land to the Northward of Cape Jakan in Siberia. But the fog was very thick, and we did not see it. A barrier of ice stopped our further progress.

The land discovered by H.B.M. Ship Herald to the Northward of Herald Island was not seen by us; we ran over its position on the English Chart, published by the Admiralty; and found only water.

As your Government has manifested a great deal of interest in the land to the Northward of Siberia I have thought you might be pleased to know how far we went.

On the 13th of August 1855 we were in Latitude 72° 05′ North, Longitude 174° 37′ West from Greenwich. On the 19th of August 1855 we were in Latitude 70° 41′ North. Longitude 177° 21′ East from Greenwich.

Plover Islands do not exist.

We saw no land except Herald Island; which was ascended.

I beg you to accept the assurances of my highest consideration, with which

I have the honor to be

> Your Excellency's
> Obedient Servant,
>
> JOHN RODGERS
> Commanding U.S. Surveying Expedition
> to the North Pacific Ocean, China Seas,
> and Behrings Straits.

To His Excellency
Nicolas Mauravieff
Governor General of
Siberia

The expedition's itinerary in northern waters is outlined in the introduction and in the reports which follow below.

Commander Rodgers reported from Petropavlovsk, July 10, 1855, that the flagship had arrived there on the eighth, to be joined on the next day by the *Fenimore Cooper*. This dispatch to Secretary Dobbin has been omitted as have Rodgers' orders to Acting Lieutenant Gibson, dated July 12th.

On August 6th, the flag officer wrote at Glassenappe Harbor informing Acting Lieutenant John M. Brooke that he and a small party would be left near a village named Yai-nang-gai, on the Siberian side of Bering Strait to make observations for magnetism and geographical position.

After the squadron had assembled at San Francisco, the botanist, Charles Wright, reported to Commander Rodgers on collections between his departure from Hongkong and July 6, 1855. About the same time (October 16th), the zoologist, William Stimpson, reported on specimens he had obtained. At the end of the month Rodgers received and forwarded a report on a botanical collection made by a certain James Small during the cruise of the *John Hancock*.

U.S. Ship Vincennes
San Francisco
Oct. 19, 1855

[Secretary Dobbin]

Sir!

I have the honor to inform you that we arrived here safely from Behrings Straits on the 13th inst.

I wrote to you from Petropaulowski, and I now beg leave to forward a statement of our operations since then.

Soon after leaving Hakodadi in Japan, we entered a region of fogs which extend[s] far into the Arctic Sea. The general obscuration of the land, and of the heavenly bodies, renders surveying results in any given time comparatively meager. The Russians complain that a vessel may cruize for a whole season and do no valuable work. It is easily understood. The currents render it impossible for a ship to hold for any long time a position near land which is invisible, and when the opportunities of observing do come, they find the laborer in a place far different from the one he desired. When he regains his position, the fog may have hidden every thing.

From these causes, a steamer is the only fit vessel to survey in such seas. We have therefore reason for congratulating ourselves, should our results prove valuable, or satisfactory.

I hope to forward to you before we leave port the charts of which a list is appended—No. 2.

On the 1st of August we entered Behrings Straits. We had passed between St. Lawrence Island, and Cape Tchaplin, in a thick fog without seeing land.

We hauled in for Leniavine Straits on the Asiatic side, where I had determined to leave a party in charge of Actg. Lt. Brooke, to make astronomical and other observations. In the afternoon we suddenly saw land close on board without our knowing exactly where we were, for we had had no observations. After several attempts to gain the harbor which were frustrated by the fogs intercepting the view of our track, in which eyesight was necessary to safety, we reached the harbor of Glassenappe. The fog then shut out the land little more than a cable length distant. The Tchuckchis, a race still unconquered and untributary, crowded around us in their skin boats. There were on board at once, some 75 men. They are a fine looking race with a very bold and free bearing. They were all dressed in furs, generally with coats of dressed deer skin, and pantaloons of sealskin.

It was with a good deal of anxiety that I determined to leave here Actg. Lieut Brooke, the two Naturalists, Messrs. [William] Stimpson and [Charles] Wright, and Mr. [Edward] Kern, the Artist, to obtain results in their respective departments, with a boats crew of five sailors and three marines, as a guard. The site of their camp having been selected, it was fortified as well as our means and time allowed. Empty provision barrels, filled with earth were placed close together around their sleeping place, and a trench dug, throwing the earth upon the barrels. Over these, a house was made of spare spars and canvass, and tents for instruments were pitched. The field piece was landed, and in the marked prudence and firmness of Mr. Brooke I had a strong assurance that I should find the party safe upon my return from the North.

On the 9th of August we passed St. Lawrence Island, and on the 11th we entered the Arctic Sea.

I had determined that our field of labor as pointed out in my instructions, was rather to the Southward of East Cape than North of it. We had but few months provisions, and fuel for even less time. It was utterly impossible that we should winter successfully at the North. Every one must needs fall a victim to protracted cold and starvation. I fixed the limits of our cruize in my own mind, and having reached them if we could, determined to return as soon as possible, in order to take up our more legitimate and useful work.

The points at which I aimed were the land in Lat about 72° North, and Long, 175° West, placed upon the Admiralty charts from a report by H. B. M.'s Frigate Herald, to examine, if possible, Plover Island, seen by the same vessel, but which he had not been able to reach, and there to endeavour to reach Wrangels land as described to him by the natives, as sometimes seen in very clear winter weather from Cape Jakan.

We were favored with a strong breeze but the weather was thick and lowering. We ran on under all sail, getting a cast of the lead every hour. On the 12th of August we came across a stream of drift timber; some of the trees were large and they were so numerous that the vessel going 7 knots had continually to alter her course to avoid striking them.

We passed over the tail of Heral[d] shoal but had no less than 18 fathoms water. On the 13th of Aug. we passed Herald Island, seen dimly between clouds. It appeared like two small islands.

The weather became very foggy. We stood to the Nd. until we had run through the position of the land in Lat 72° North, Long 175° West which we found given on the admiralty charts and we came to anchor with the hemp stream in 42 fathoms water, soft blue mud, in Lat 72° 05′ Long 174° 37′ W. In a few hours the fog lifted and a sudden change, peculiar I believe to Northern Seas, flashed across the scene. It was so clear that our horizon was apparently without limit. No land nor appearance of land could be seen from the Royal

[138]

yards. The water was as far as the eye could reach entirely free from ice.

The weather again became foggy. We had accomplished what I had proposed to myself and we returned towards Herald Island. On the evening of the 14th of Aug. we judged ourselves near the Island we sought, and we came to in a thick fog with the stream anchor. At night we heard the surf breaking sullenly on the shores and at 2 in the morning an avalanche thundered down the sides of the Island, which we had not seen. At 6 we were enabled to leave the vessel in two boats. Unluckily the heavens were obscured and our observations were not satisfactory. Those which we did obtain were taken from the vessel. The circumstances were somewhat unfavorable to accuracy.

The position we assigned to Herald Island differs from that given by Capt. Kellet, whose opportunities were perhaps even less good than ours. The Vincenne's position of Herald Island is for its S.E. point, 71°. 21′. N. Lat. 175°, 20′. W. Long.

The Island is in the form of a half moon, and its horns are connected by a less elevated isthmus, which gives sometimes the appearence of there being two Islands, for the isthmus may be below the horizon, while the extremes are above it.

The sides of the Island were very steep and the ascent was full of danger. John Watts, one of the boats crew, a very active man and of good eyesight, was sent to attempt getting to the top. He succeeded, but an Officer who also attempted it was near losing his life, from a piece of rock giving way under his foot. The difficulty of the ascent consisted in the friable nature of the soil. The frost had broken the materials of the Island until the rocks and earth gave only a very treacherous foot hold.

From the summit of Herald Island no land could be seen in any direction. The horizon had now become good. From the Royal yards our hopes of seeing land were equally frustrated.

It would be far pleasanter to confirm the discovery of other land than Herald Island, than to believe that Capt. Kellet was mistaken in his views. Yet we were convinced, however unwillingly, that appearances had deceived him. Several times land was reported by men at the mast head, which eventually proved to be only clouds, and sometimes where I knew no land could be, since we had passed through the position in which it was said to lie.

On the 15th of Aug. We ran for Plover Island; the air was clear and bracing. We stood in the direction of Plover Islands, but when half way to their position on the chart were stopped by a barrier of ice. We were half the distance from them which the Herald had been and the weather was favorable for seeing them, did they really exist. From the Royal yards nothing like land could be discovered. I am forced to the conclusion that the Plover Islands do not exist—Here too Capt. Kellet was mislead by appearances. He could only give his honest convictions. It would have been wrong to omit the notice of such palpable appearances as deceived him. He could not approach more nearly. Any navigator must under circumstances such as controlled his act follow his course of giving his honest convictions, and then he must leave the matter for the investigation of time and for confirmation or rejection by those who shall have better opportunities for ascertaining the truth of what he saw was probable.—

We tacked near the edge of the barrier and stood to the Sd. We ran for Wrangels land. On the 19th of Aug. the weather was very foggy. Continuous ice was reported. Walruses were blowing around us, and masses of ice were floating near. We had a wall like barrier before us. We could not go farther. We had arrived within ten miles of the position of Wrangels land, never seen by European eyes, nor did we discover it. A fog hid every thing. Yet it was not so thick but that we thought we could see some six or eight miles in every direction.

It was with a certain reluctance that I had resolved to run for this land, for the time I should thus occupy was so much taken from the peculiar duties imposed. I knew however that no keel had penetrated where I proposed to go, and the depths and temperatures and currents would be of value even should I fail of discovering land.

We were in the reputed Polynia Lat. 70° 41′ N. Long. 177° 21′ E. Or always open water of the Russians. Ice was floating in it only however when we reached the barrier, which may have rested on land. It was uncertain how long we should have to wait for clear weather. I had no time to spare and I gave orders to return.

We had attained the limits I had proposed. We had penetrated farther than any one else in the direction I had selected and if we failed to discover land, it was because the sea within those limits at least bore none. After that we were annoyed with continual head winds blowing from the NE.

On the 31st of Aug. We rounded East Cape going 11½ knots under all sail with every appearance of a gale. We ran into St. Lawrence Bay, which we surveyed. We left St. Lawrence Bay on the 3d of Septbr, and on the 5th we anchored at Leniavine where we were delighted to find our little party under Mr. Brooke quite safe and in excellent health.

We left Leniavine Straits on the 17th of September. On the 24th passed through the Aleutian chain by the Straits of Amoukta, at night. The passage is an excellent one to be recommended to all navigators through these seas as the widest and as possibly the best. On the 13th of October arrived here without any thing remarkable having occurred during the passage.

I have the honor to be

Very Respectfully

Your Obedient Servant

JOHN RODGERS
Comdg. U.S. Surveying Expedition
to the North Pacific Ocean &c.

Honorable James C. Dobbin
Secretary of the Navy
Washington, D.C.

(The reports of the Hancock and Cooper both of which vessels are in port are enclosed.)

U.S. Schooner Fenimore Cooper
San Francisco
Octr. 11th, 1855

[Secretary of the Navy Dabbin]
Sir:

Having reached this port in advance of the Vincennes, I have instructions from Lieut. Comdg. Rodgers, anticipating the event, to report directly to the Department.

I have therefore the honor to inform you that this vessel left Petropaulaski on the 16th of July, the Vincennes having sailed for the Arctic two days previous.

Since then we have made reconnaissance of the Aleutian islands with a degree of completeness which in that region of prevailing tempest and fog has exceeded my most sanguine hopes. We have determined in latitude and connected in a chain of chronometric differences all the principal islands except one (Agattou) not seen and most of the smaller islets and rocks of that archipelago; the passages between the islands have been carefully examined; the heights of many peaks and headlands measured, numerous points triangulated and shore lines traced, and several harbors surveyed.

If any hope should yet linger in regard to the fate of the officers and crew of the Whale Ship Monongahela, I am grieved that what I have to report must forever extinguish it. No part of my instructions was I more solicitous to fulfill than the search and inquiry after survivors from that vessel. I communicated with the Superintendent of the Russian American Company's settlement on the island of Atcka. At that place are still several water casks supposed to have belonged to the Monongahela and I have in my possession a gilt cabin moulding obtained there. Fragments of a wreck or wrecks

[142]

have been picked up on the shores of Amla, Atcka, and Kossatotchy islands from the winter of 1853-54—up to some time in the current year.

The constant communication by bäidars[58] with all parts of Amla and Atcka and also with the islands closely grouped to the westward of Atcka makes it impossible that any ship-wrecked crew can be there at this late day. Hearing that since the fall of 1853 no intelligence had been received at Atcka from the islands of Sigouam and Amoughta which lie one on each side of the 72d passage, I ran closely along their shores. Off Amoughta we fell in with a number of Creole and Aleutian fishermen, from whom my information was positive that there were no wrecked mariners on Amoughta or on its neighbouring islands Tscheqoula and Una[la]ska. Neither were there any on Segouam which they had visited before coming to Amoughta. This, coupled with our own coasting examination in that vicinity, forces the melancholy conclusion that all on board the Monongahela perished with her.

At Attou, the first Aleutian island in our track, I heard of the loss of the New Bedford on the Semichi islands in 1852. A few of her crew had been for a time at Port Tschitchagoff, and had left in a passing whaler which they pulled off a bäidar. The Company's Superintendent there knew nothing of the Monongahela.

From the Aleutian islands we proceeded via the Choumagine group to the port of New Archangel in Sitka, where we arrived on the 19th of September. From Governor Veovodsky I obtained a statement of all the information in his Excellency's possession relative to the loss of a vessel in the fall of 1853 near the Aleutian island of Atcka. A copy is herewith forwarded as also a copy and translation of a paper of similar purport, made for me in the Russian language by the Superintendent at Atcka. The gilt lettering of a vessel's name being taken on board a Rus. Am. Comp.'y's Brig "Ochotsck" as stated in these pages has doubtless been the means by which

---

[58] A type of canoe.

the wreck is identified at home; but both at Sitka and at Atcka the name of the Monongahela was unknown.

In my instructions from Lieut. Comdg. Rodgers the search after coal was especially enjoined upon me. Whenever it was practicable personally to seek or to visit localities where it was reported to be I did so, but I found nothing but fossil wood more or less coaly in appearance. Out of specimens which I succeeded in obtaining from places which we were unable ourselves to visit, I have but one of genuine coal. This, and a piece of pure copper, were brought from Copper island by the priest of Atcka, who kindly gave them to me.

I hear from good authority that there is coal near the NW extremity of the island of Amtschitka. Of the nature or extent of it I have not been able to gain any knowledge.

The Coal beds on the bay of Zackharoff Island of Ounga were worked for a while but are so no longer. The coal was found to be valueless, containing much sulphur.

Coal, of excellent quality and in great abundance, exists in various places along Cook's inlet.

His Excellency the Governor of the Rus. Colonies in America cordially furnished me with the Company's charts with meteorological and title tables and with whatever of interest the hydrographical office at New Archangel afforded. From the officers of the settlement generally vying in friendly endeavours I obtained orally and otherwise much information of value. Nor did curtesies and kindnesses stop here. As American officers attached to the first U.S. vessel which had visited Sitka, no welcome could be warmer. And it is with grateful pleasure that I find this early opportunity of reporting to the Department our obligations.

I have the honor to be,

Very respectfully,
Your obdt. Servt.

WILLIAM GIBSON
Actg. Lieut. Comdg.

[Commander Rodgers]

Sir:

I have the honor to report that according to your instructions, having finished the examination of the Straits of "Isugar" or Sangar, We sailed from there on the 4th of July last and proceeded along the west coast of "Jesso" or "Matsmai," following the shore closely as far as the Straits of La Perouse.

No part of the coast escaped us, and as we anchored every night, with but one exception our work is well connected though on some days we were unable to get observations. Capes Romanzoff, and Soya at the North end of Jesso have been landed on, and their positions well determined. The Islands have all been located on passing them, and Refunchery, which has an extensive chain of rocks off its North end, has been reconnoitered, while the whole shore line has been carefully sketched in by Mr. Hartman the Draftsman. We are thus enabled to give a complete chart of that coast. We then crossed the Straits to visit Cape Geillon, and the rock situated off of it, but a very heavy fog prevented our seeing the land. And after a days delay, we stood on to Cape "Aniva," the position of which was fixed by good observations from the ship, when quite near it. Everywhere we found the determinations of Krusenstern very correct, but his outline of the land is often faulty: and in some places native names have been misapplied. Leaving Cape Aniva on the 16th of July, we started across for Kamschatka and made the coast in the neighborhood of the River "Solsha" Lat. 53 N., but owing to a fog which obscured the land for a short time, we passed the entrance without seeing it. From there however we traced the shore closely up as far as Cape Omegan, but after leaving that cape we had some thick weather which caused some of the deeper indentations to escape us: Still all the prominent points were fixed and the shore line generally traced in as far as Lat. 60° 55′ on the East side of the Gulf of Penjinsk; which is as high as we went. In 60° 18′ we found an abundance of coal, and as we had been obliged to use ours freely in order to get along, it became necessary to replenish our stock from the mines. Accordingly having anchored there on the 30th of July, we succeeded through the untiring exertions of all hands, in taking in 45 tons of coal by the morning of the 4th of August, and on the 5th we sailed. The conduct of the men in completing this piece of work as they did is above praise, and to Mr. Lawton, who assisted by Mr. Squires, superintended digging the coal, great credit is due for the energy and zeal displayed in carrying out the work. Sailing on the 5th of August, we proceeded to the Nd. but having both wind and current against us, we made very little progress. The next day we visited another coal mine and succeeded in reaching Lat. 60° 55′ N. We saw but little of the West side of this Gulf, but passed close round Cape Toinotskoi, which separates from the Gulf of Tijiginsk. From Cape Toinotskoi we stood directly across to the Westd. and then along that shore to the Gulf of Jamsk. The mouth of this Gulf was passed during the night, as time could not be spared to examine it, for I deemed it necessary to hurry to the Sd. We however landed next day on the South Side of it and got observations to fix the Long. along this part of the coast, which was found very incorrect. The Group of Islands off the east end of this promontory was examined and then we followed the shore along to Tanisk Bay. This Bay being much frequented by whalers, I deemed it particularly deserving of examination, and therefore devoted several days to which I believe was a good employment of the time. Here too, we were obliged to take in some water which occupied us two days, So that notwithstanding all diligence was used, It was the 25th of August before we finally left the Bay. We then attempted to follow the land to the Wd. but the weather was very unfavorable: we still however succeeded in sighting all the Head lands as far as Long 145° 30′ E. I wished to connect this examination with some known point about Ochotsk, but it came on to blow hard with thick weather which caused me to keep away at once for Jonas Island, the position of which I wished to test. We made it on the 29th of August in the morning, and I flattered myself that we were going to have a good day for our work, but a thick fog set in before any observations could be obtained, and gave us no chance throughout the day, though we waited near the spot in hopes of its clearing off. In the evening we stood for Ayan where we arrived on the evening of the 31st. We found the place deserted by the inhabitants on account of the visits of the English and French: but I met the agent of the Russian Fur Co. there, and also the Governor before I left. Both offered all in their power to promote the objects of the expedition. From the Agent in Fryburg I received in the name of his government a book of charts which he said contained all of their recent surveys that had been published. In return I gave him a set of wind & current charts and some of the coast survey sheets to be presented to his government from ours.

A survey of the Harbor of Ayan was made and observations obtained for rates, and on the 5th of September we sailed again. At first we kept along the land to the SWd. in hopes of finding a coal mine reported to be somewhere between Lat. 55° 40′ & 55° 50′ N. Nothing however was seen of it, we then stretched across for the Tschantar Islands, & passing along the West side of Feklister, entered the Bay on its South side. Here we found several whalers & some of them having coal to spare I was induced to anchor in hopes of getting some. But the only one that had any quantity, after having promised to let me have it, came & begged off as it would take him two days to break it out of his lower hold & he was only waiting for a wind to go to sea. Being thus disappointed, I devoted a day to cutting wood, & by using all the boats I succeeded in getting off 10 cords. In the mean time the position of the bay was determined by observations on shore. The whaling Captains gave me such accounts of the bad weather about the Gulf of Saghalien in September, that I was forced to conclude the proper season for working there has already past. Still I determined to push on down there as fast as possible & have a look at it for myself. We accordingly sailed on the 9th but had hardly got outside the Bay before it came on to blow from the Nd. with thick rainy weather. I therefore ran under the lee of Great Tschantar & anchored in the Bay on its south side. It continued to blow in heavy squalls all that day until the next evening when it commenced to moderate. The next morning, Sept. 11, we got underway, & passing out between Great & Little Tschantar, stood across to Cape Muchtochija, where night over took us. Running on to the Ed. we were up with Reineke Is. in the morning, & from there we traced the shore closely to the entrance of the Gulf of Saghalien. On the 13th while standing into the Gulf, we overhauled a Russian Launch & learned from an officer on board of her that there was undoubtedly a passage through to the Gulf of Tartary, since all these vessels had passed through it from Cartusbury to the Amour where they now were, & he was then bound into the river himself. He also mentioned that a schooner had circumnavigated Saghalien, stating however that the channel was narrow & in some places had only 16 feet of water in it. On learning that we wished to go into the river, he said that the season was too late to do much then, that the middle of September (old style) was the latest period that the navigation of the gulf was considered safe. I gave some weight to his opinion, as he had been living for 5 years at "Petrosky," situated just at the entrance of the Gulf. We were then in 5 fath water with the breakers close aboard to the Sd. & an extensive line of Breakers to the Nd. seeming to reach all the way to the Saghalien shore, which was seen in the distance to the Ed. Under the land to the Ed. we discovered an American vessel, & believing that we could float where she did, I pushed on for her. She proved to be the Barque "Palmetto" from San Francisco, bound into the Amour. She had been there ten days trying to get in. Having a pilot & being assisted by a number of Russian Naval boats. We were taken for an English vessel & all the boats left her as we approached, but on our hoisting a white flag they returned, and as soon as the Russian officers understood who we were & that we wished to go into the river, an officer was despatched to inform the Admiral. At the same time they recommended that I should not attempt the passage until an answer was received, which they said they expected back the next evening. This I readily agreed to & accordingly anchored near the Palmetto in 3 and ¾ faths just in the mouth of the Gulf, or more properly the *straits*. On board of the Palmetto I saw a chart of the straits, but the Russians were much annoyed at my having got hold of it, & after my visit it disappeared. This chart showed a channel passing directly through the straits having a branch from each entrance leading to the mouth of the Amour. A wide bar just opposite the mouth of the river with only 16 feet of water on it obstructed the main channel which in other parts had a depth of from 4 to 12 faths & was generally about a mile & a half wide. The branches also had their bars, & all the space between the channels was filled with banks & extensive flats.

Sept. 14 & the morning of the 15th were employed in sounding: which showed us that we were in a narrow channel, & with sand Banks on each side of us. While I was away in the morning I noticed a couple of Russian boats come down the river and the Palmetto get under way, but soon after she suddenly anchored again. It seemed that they had started expecting to run down in the main channel, but finding that they were steering directly onto the bank, they had anchored just in time to save grounding. On my return I found that the Captain of a Corvette had arrived & called on me. I therefore immediately returned his visit on board the Palmetto. From him I learned that the Officer could not get back before the evening of the 17th & the Admiral had gone up the river some distance, which might make it still longer before I heard from him. This officer had been told that I wished to get a copy of the chart of the straits, but he said it was impossible to let me have it, as it was a secret. I now gave up entirely the idea of making the passage through the Straits, for from what I had seen & all that I could learn, I was satisfied that in order to accomplish any useful results we should have to devote more time to it than we could afford to do then. Little or no aid could be expected from the Russians, even if they granted permission for us to go into the Amour, as I should be obliged to find the channel with my own boats: which in such shoal water, the slightest rough weather would prevent anything being done. Moreover I deemed the object to be gained incommensurate with the risk of the vessel among those shoals during the coming Equinox. Having come to this conclusion I believed that we could not leave the Gulf too soon, for the Barometer had commenced falling, with thick weather coming on, So that one days delay might cause our detention until bad weather set in. I therefore wrote a letter to Rear Admiral Zavoika Commander in Chief of the Russian Naval forces at the Amour, a copy of which is herewith enclosed, & on the 16th of September we sailed. It was fortunate we delayed no longer, for though we had the short passage of 33 days our bread all gave out before we got in, all the rice & beans we had were unfit for issue, & the flour would have lasted only a few days longer, so that it was with high satisfaction that we made the land on the 18th of October, & got in that night.

In this I have endeavored to give you a summary account of our cruise, but I shall soon make a more detailed report of our work. Mr. Hartman has labored hard & will soon now be able to bring up everything, but from the nature of our work he has been so constantly employed in sketching on the shore that it was impossible for him to keep up the plotting at the same time. I am under the necessity of reporting that this vessel will require a good deal of work done to her before she can be fitted for another cruise. In the first place the boilers leak badly & will require to be lifted or taken out, so as to get at the bottom part of them, there not being space enough to work between them & the Kelsons. At the same time all the tubes require to be examined, & perhaps a complete new set put in. A new smoke stack, & new feed pipe, with some other piping will have to be made, & the propeller shaft taken out, as the water is leaking between the casing & shaft. Then the vessel herself leaks, so as not only to make cabin ward Room & berth deck uncomfortable, but to require pumping regularly 3 times a day & if blowing fresh every watch: this increased leakage has been principally during the last 2 weeks. My impression is that it is mainly owing to her want of proper Knees: her extreme length causing her to twist herself, & work very much in a sea way.

In conclusion I beg to recommend both officers & crew to your favorable notice, for their constant exertions during so arduous a cruise.

I am very Respectfully
Your Obt. Svt.

H. K. Stevens
Lt. Comdg.

To Lieut. John Rodgers
Comdg. Expedition to
North Pacific &c &c.
U.S.S. Vincennes
San Francisco.

U.S. Steamer John Hancock
Navy Yard
Mare Island
November 2nd, 1855.

[Commander Rodgers]
Sir!

Other occupations have prevented my finishing my hydrographical report, but I deem it expedient to make known to you as soon as possible some of the particular wants of our Mercantile and Whaling marine, which have struck me during the cruise, but which my limited time forced me to leave unattended to.

First then, It is highly important that the Kurile islands

should be well examined, as the Whalers not only push through the first available passage in the spring, but return in July to cruize along the Western side of the group.

They report that the Southern islands are very incorrectly charted and that some of them are as much as a degree further to the Eastrd than the charts place them. Two whale ships were lost in the north end of Ouroup this spring, having sighted the Southern end of the island the day before, and steering as they thought, to clear every thing.

For the same reasons, the North side of "Jesso," or Matsmai, requires to be surveyed, and if possible, a port in that neighbourhood opened for our whalers, who pass along its shores in July, and would be able to supply themselves with a few refreshments that could not be found on the Kamtschatka coast, which is their next cruising ground. Secondly, Both the approaches to the River "Amour" require a good examination, and the river itself visited, not so much for the purpose of surveying its channel which would be useless, as it is subject to constant changes, but to obtain information with regard to the resources of the country and the wants of the people, for I am persuaded that a useful commerce may be established in provisions and other necessaries with that place. And it will be one of the links in our Japanese and Chinese trade, for whatever the fertility of the soil on the banks of the Amour or its tributaries, it will avail little to the Russians through want of laborers for sometime to come, and every thing may be more cheaply obtained from our country than from the interior of Russia, thus that country producing nothing to make a return cargo, would supply money, which in a few days would be laid out to advantage in Japan, or if preferred, in China.

San Francisco is particularly interested in this, and through San Francisco, all our country.

Thirdly: Our whalers require a more particular survey of the bays to the Southrd of the Tshantu Islands and of the islands themselves. I was lead to believe that the Russian charts of these places were all sufficient, but my slight investigation showed that there was much yet to be done.

Our Whalers have heretofore been compelled to depend so much on their own resources and have forced their way into so many unknown waters that they hardly realize the advantage of good charts, but if a chart were given them by which they could recognize the land and tell at once their position, it would soon be appreciated.

Latitude and Longitude are of less importance to them while on cruising ground than a knowledge of the coast line and of the bottom, with a correct idea of the currents, for much of the time they are close along the shore enveloped in fog, or among ice, so that few observations are taken, and they have to trust for their safety to the lead and look-out.

Among the Tshantu Islands the bottom is so bad in some places that two anchors with 100 fathoms of chain on each have been found insufficient to hold a vessel. Again, off Petrosky, an anchor let go in a blow can seldom be recovered, as it sinks so deeply in a kind of quicksand; Still there are places where good anchorage can be had.

Fourthly, There is a bay situated about Lat. 59° 10′ N. and Long, 145° 45′ E. according to the Russian Charts, which is reported to possess a harbour, and be frequented by Whales, but our Whalers know very little of it.

Further surveys are also required in the Gulfs of Jamsk, Jijiginsk, and Penjinsk. It is also highly desirable to have the River Solsha, and harbour of Bolcharetsk, situated about Lat. 52° 50′ N. and 156° E, examined. I find no plan of it among the Russian charts, and as our Whalers seek the Right Whale in that neighbourhood in the last part of the season, a knowledge of the harbour might be useful to them.

All this work can only be done efficiently by a steamer. Lastly, I would suggest to our Government the expediency of having a Consular Agent at the Russian port of Ayan, to reside there at least during the Whaling season.

Over one hundred of our vessels are cruising in that vicinity every year, and perhaps two thirds of them look in at Ayan. These vessels are peculiarly liable to accident from the many dangers they encounter, while in case of damage, Ayan is the only place within a long distance at which succour can be had. Last year several vessels availed themselves of that friendly port to repair injuries that might have caused their loss, but for the timely aid they received.

The Russian Fur Company, have a Hospital there too, into which arrangements might be made to have seamen admitted, where they would have kind attention, and many comforts, instead of languishing for months, and months, as they do now, on board of their vessels, without the aid of a doctor. Some special law should also require a Captain to land his sick men if they require it, for without that, the interest of the voyage will often outweigh the interest of humanity. . . .

H. K. STEVENS
Lieut. Comdg.

To Lieut. John Rodgers.
Comdg. Expedition to
North Pacific, &c.
U.S. Ship Vincennes.

U.S. Ship Vincennes
San Francisco
October 19th, 1855

List of Charts made by the U.S. Surveying Expedn. to the North Pacific Ocean ectr since last April and at present, ready to be sent home or in preparation.

I. Finished or nearly so:

1. Harbor of Simoda ⎫ in Japan.
2. " " Hakodadi ⎭
3. Harbor of Petropaulawski and the Bay of Awatska with the adjoining coast of Kamschatka.
4. St. Lawrence Bay in Behrings Straits.
5. Herald Island in the Arctic Ocean.

BY THE U.S. SHIP VINCENNES

6. S.W, S. and S.E. Coast of Formosa.
7. Part of the East Coast of Formosa.
8. The Amakarima Group near Loo Choo.
9. Montgommery Islands, near Loo Choo.
10. Parts of Ousima.
11. Fatsisio Island ectr, Japan.
12. Coast from Simoda to Hedi, Japan.
13. Straits of Sangar between Niphon and Jesso.

BY THE STEAMER JOHN HANCOCK

II. In preparation,

14. Straits of Leniavine (Behrings Sts.)
15. Behrings Straits.
16. Arctic Sea.
17. West Coast of Jesso, Japan, by the Hancock.

BY THE VINCENNES

III. There remains to be plotted:

18. Loo-Choo, from original work and information procured.

19. Additions to the Chain of Islands between Loo Choo and Ousima.

20. West Coast of Ousima with three harbors and additions to the East Coast.

21. Additions to the chain of Islands between Ousima & Kiusiu.

} BY THE VINCENNES AND THE FENIMORE COOPER

22. East Coast of Niphon by the Launch OF THE VINCENNES.

23. West Coast of Kiusiu and Niphon.

24. East Coast of Jesso.

} BY THE COOPER

25. Aleutian Group and Schoumagin Island BY THE COOPER.

26. West Coast of St. Lawrence Island BY THE VINCENNES.

27. South Side of the Straits of La Perouse.

28. Cape Arniva & adjacent coast, North side of Straits of La Perouse.

29. West Coast of Kamschatka.

30. North shore of the Sea of Ochotsk.

31. S.W. & South Part of Sea of Ochotsk.

32. Northern approaches to the River Amour.

} BY THE JOHN HANCOCK

Very Respectfully,
JOHN RODGERS
Commanding U.S. Surv. Expedn. to the North Pacific Ocean

U.S. Ship Vincennes,
Mare Island Navy Yard, Cal.,
[Secretary Dobbin]   December 3rd, 1855.

Sir,

I scarcely know how to write in relation to a fear, which as I do not know that it has any foundation, seems rather to address your private ear than your official one.

I had the honor to send you from Hong Kong a parcel of charts of our work. I have not heard anything of them. I apprehend that they may have fallen into the hands of Capt. Ringgold.

A confirmation of this apprehension would be so great an evil to me that I loose my equanimity in thinking of it.

These charts were the fruits of many month's labor under circumstances which I regarded as difficult. To me they stood in place of other proof that I was not unworthy of the honor I might receive from you, of confirmation in my position. I have not the good fortune to admire Capt. Ringgold, either in his morals or in his intellect. It is doubtless because I do not know him better.

My ignorance then of his character, and my knowledge that he bears me illwill, suggest fears which I hope he is incapable of deserving.

Nothing but necessity would compel me to use the means which I may have to prevent his fashioning my labors. I wrote a letter in answer to his applications for the Gaspar Straits work, which after several days deliberation I am induced to supress, in the hope that he does not receive the papers of the Expedition and prepare their contents.

To you the matter of his letter appears trivial, yet your philosophy will tell, having been earnest in making them, it is most natural I should be earnest in their preservation.

I hope you may deem my earnestness even not ungraceful; since I have succeeded to the position I hold under your auspices, and zeal is a necessary foundation to active merit; so far it is commendable.

When you receive those charts, let me beg that you will hand them over to the Bureau of Hydrography, to be prepared by Lieutenant Maury of the National Observatory.

I have the honor to be

Your obdt servt,

(signed) JOHN RODGERS
Comdg. Surveying Expedition

Honorable James C. Dobbin
Secretary of the Navy
Washington, D.C.

Again Commander Rodgers wrote to his superior from San Francisco on January 26, 1856, saying that he was ordering Lieutenant John M. Brooke to Washington for scientific work connected with preparing materials which had been collected by the expedition. Lieutenant Brooke received his instructions on the same day. As recounted in the introduction, this scientist worked at the Naval Observatory from March to October, 1856. Then, still under orders from Commander Rodgers, he prepared to assume command of the *Fenimore Cooper* and of that unfinished phase of the expedition, the charting of a prospective steamship route between the Golden Gate and China's commercial coast. This was accomplished in 1858, and thus the major objectives of the United States Surveying Expedition to the North Pacific Ocean were completed.

Navy Department[59]
December 5th 1855.

Sir,

The fund appropriated by Congress for the Survey of Behrings Straits, North Pacific Ocean and China Seas has long since been exhausted; You state that the vessels under your command are short of the number of officers necessary for you to carry out successfully your future plans of Survey—to supply the officers you desire (even if they were available) would involve the Department in a great expense. From these considerations and the fact that you have executed so well the

[59] This letter is to be found in Confidential Letters, No. 3, February 1, 1853, to October 17, 1857 (MS).

Surveys which were specially authorized by Congress, the Department is induced to put an end to the Expedition.

It is considered unnecessary to bring the Fenimore Cooper to the Atlantic Coast. You will therefore transfer her officers crew and stores (if any) to the Vincennes and you will turn the vessel over to the Yard. You will then with the Vincennes proceed to New York by such route as you may deem advisable informing the Department by the course of mail of your intentions.

I avail myself of this occasion to assure you of my high appreciation of the energy and industry displayed by yourself and officers and of the Successful manner in which you have performed your duties. Make known to the officers and crew also this favorable opinion of the Department.

I am respectfully,

Your Obt Servt,

J. C. DOBBIN

Comr John Rodgers
Commg U.S. North Pacific Expedition &c.,
San Francisco, Cal.

U.S. Ship Vincennes
San Francisco, California
January 29th 1856.

[Secretary Dobbin]

Sir!

I have the honor to acknowledge the receipt of your letter of December 5th, containing the announcement of your satisfaction at our efforts, and assuring me to make it known to the officers and crew.

An expression of Official Satisfaction is very dear to the heart of a Naval man, His Chief is to him the fountain of honor, and the hope of winning approbation, cheers him in hours of difficulty or privation.

It has been with a sentiment of . . . military pride that your enconium has been read at "General Muster."

I have determined in using the discretion you have so kindly given, to return to the Atlantic by the way of Cape Horn.

An island has been reported to lie in Latitude 40° 40′ N, and in about Longitude 150°, 50′ West. The report wears an appearance of authenticity. Should it accidentily contain a harbor, its examination before it has been landed upon or taken possession of may have political importance. In any case it is of consequence to know of its position. The probability is that this Island has no harbor; it is possible that it has a fine one. We shall look for it.

From the Sandwich Islands we shall proceed South, touching at Otaheite, Thence on a Great Circle round Cape Horn and probably touching at Rio Janeiro, make the best of our way to New York.

In our passage through the Dangerous Archipelago, our observations will not be without interest for commerce.

Little afterwards remains, except meteorological observations and deep sea soundings.

It is perhaps to be regretted that circumstances have rendered it inexpedient to survey the route to China immediately. Its importance is in my opinion very great. A proper survey would, by pointing out the position of real dangers and by crossing imaginary ones from the Chart, enable the navigator to sail boldly where he now passes with great anxiety, and under reduced sail.

I think that the Pacific Rail Road, and Steamers to China, will turn the tide of commerce this way.[60] We shall carry to Europe their teas and silk, from New York. I believe that this result is inevitable; and I also think the time of its attainment will be shortened by accelerating as far as possible the passage to China.

The results are so vast as to dazzle sober calculation; and in gazing at so gorgeous a future, I may readily have over

[60] The trans-continental railroad was completed in 1869; a trans-Pacific steamship line was first inaugurated in 1867.

valued the importance of a survey which is to accelerate its coming.

By far the greater part of the Charts in use by navigators have been made by the English. We, through California, inherit the trade of the Pacific; for we are the only nation upon it which cultivates foreign commerce. In the Pacific we can scarcely hope that the English will make charts, from which we must reap so much more advantage than they. Self interest would rather counsel their putting an impassable barrier, were it possible, between our country and China.

I hold then, that the route to China must be surveyed by the United States. The outlay can not be avoided.

In saying thus much, I hope you will consider me as giving an opinion derived from studying the hydrographic problem, Ex officio submitted to me. My sense of its importance has been quickened by seeing the wonderful energy of California, and her progress under its influence.

I have the honor to be

Very Respectfully

Your Obedient Servant,

JOHN RODGERS
Commanding U.S. Surveying Expedition to the North Pacific Ocean, &c.

Honorable James C. Dobbin,
Secretary of the Navy,
Washington, D.C.